THE COLLECTED
WORKS OF
RAMANA
MAHARSHI

THE COLLECTED WORKS OF RAMANA MAHARSHI

Edited by Arthur Osborne

SAMUEL WEISER, INC.

York Beach, Maine

This edition published in 1997 by
Samuel Weiser, Inc.
P. O. Box 612
York Beach, ME 03910-0612

03 02 01 00 99 98 97
10 9 8 7 6 5 4 3 2 1

Library of Congress Catalog Card Number 75 18518

ISBN 0-87728-907-7

Printed in the United States of America
CCP

The paper used in this publication meets the minimum require-
ments of the American National Standard for Permanence of
Paper for Printed Library Materials Z39.48-1984.

Contents

Preface

When the Maharshi, Bhagavan Sri Ramana, realized the Self he was a lad of seventeen in a middle-class Brahmin family of South India. He was still going to high school and had undergone no spiritual training and learnt nothing of spiritual philosophy. Normally some study is needed, followed by long and arduous training, often lasting a whole lifetime, more often still incomplete at the end of a lifetime. As the Sages say, it depends on the spiritual maturity of a person. It can be compared to a pilgrimage, and a day's journey on it to a lifetime: a person's attaining the goal, or how near he gets to it, will depend partly on the energy with which he presses forward and partly on the distance from it at which he wakes up and begins his day's journey. Only in the rarest cases is it possible, as with the Maharshi, to take a single step and the goal is reached.

To say that the Maharshi realized the Self does not mean that he understood any new doctrine or theory or achieved any higher state or miraculous powers, but that the 'I' who understands or does not understand doctrine and who possesses or does not possess powers became consciously identical with the Atman, the universal Self or Spirit. The Maharshi himself has described in simple, picturesque language how this happened.

'It was about six weeks before I left Madura for good that the great change in my life took place. It was quite sudden. I was sitting alone in a room on the first floor of my uncle's house. I seldom had any sickness, and on that day there was nothing wrong with my health, but a sudden violent fear of death overtook me. There was nothing in my state of health to account for it, and I did not try to account for it or to find out whether there

7

was any reason for the fear. I just felt "I am going to die" and began thinking what to do about it. It did not occur to me to consult a doctor or my elders or friends; I felt that I had to solve the problem myself, there and then.

The shock of the fear of death drove my mind inwards and I said to myself mentally, without actually framing the words: "Now death has come; what does it mean? What is it that is dying? This body dies." And I at once dramatized the occurrence of death. I lay with my limbs stretched out stiff as though *rigor mortis* had set in and imitated a corpse so as to give greater reality to the enquiry. I held my breath and kept my lips tightly closed so that no sound could escape, so that neither the word "I" nor any other word could be uttered. "Well then," I said to myself, "this body is dead. It will be carried stiff to the burning ground and there burnt and reduced to ashes. But with the death of this body am I dead? Is the body I? It is silent and inert but I feel the full force of my personality and even the voice of the 'I' within me, apart from it. So I am Spirit transcending the body. The body dies but the Spirit that transcends it cannot be touched by death. That means I am the deathless Spirit." All this was not dull thought; it flashed through me vividly as living truth which I perceived directly, almost without thought-process. "I" was something very real, the only real thing about my present state, and all the conscious activity connected with my body was centred on that "I". From that moment onwards the "I" or Self focused attention on itself by a powerful fascination. Fear of death had vanished once and for all. Absorption in the Self continued unbroken from that time on. Other thoughts might come and go like the various notes of music, but the "I" continued like the fundamental *sruti* note that underlies and blends with all the other notes.[1] Whether the body was engaged in talking, reading, or anything else, I was still centred on "I". Previous to that crisis I had no clear perception of my Self and was not consciously attracted to it. I felt no perceptible or direct interest in it, much less any inclination to dwell permanently in it.'

[1] The monotone persisting through a Hindu piece of music, like the thread on which beads are strung, represents the Self persisting through all the forms of being.

Such an experience of Identity does not always, or even normally, result in Liberation. It comes to a seeker but the inherent tendencies of the ego cloud it over again. Thenceforward he has the memory, the indubitable certainty, of the True State, but he does not live in it permanently. He has to strive to purify the mind and attain complete submission so that there are no tendencies to pull him back again to the illusion of limited separative being. 'However, the Self-oblivious ego, even when once made aware of the Self, does not get Liberation, that is Self-realization, on account of the obstruction of accumulated mental tendencies. It frequently confuses the body with the Self, forgetting that it is itself in truth the Self' (p. 16). The miracle was that in the Maharshi's case there was no clouding over, no relapse into ignorance; he remained thenceforward in constant awareness of identity with the One Self.

For a few weeks after this awakening he remained with his family, leading outwardly the life of a schoolboy although all outer values had lost their meaning for him. He no longer cared what he ate, accepting with like indifference whatever was offered. He no longer stood up for his rights or interested himself in boyish activities. So far as possible he conformed to the conditions of life and concealed his new state of consciousness, but his elders saw his lack of interest in learning and all worldly activities and resented it.

There are many holy places in India, representing different modes of Spirituality and different types of path. The holy hill of Arunachala with the town of Tiruvannamalai at its foot is supreme among them in that it is the centre of the direct path of Self-enquiry guided by the silent influence of the Guru upon the heart of the devotee. It is the seat of Siva who, in the form of Dakshinamurti, teaches in silence and who has been identified with Bhagavan. It is the centre and the path where physical contact with the Guru is not necessary but the silent teaching speaks direct to the heart. Even before his Realization it had thrilled the Maharshi and drawn him like a magnet.

'Hearken; It stands as an insentient[1] Hill. Its action is mysterious past human understanding. From the age of innocence it had shone within my mind that Arunachala was something of surpassing

[1] The adjective also bears the meaning 'eradicating objective knowledge'.

grandeur,[1] but even when I came to know through another that it was the same as Tiruvannamalai I did not realize its meaning. When it drew me up to it, stilling my mind, and I came close, I saw it (stand) unmoving.'[2]

Now, seeing that his elders resented his living like a sadhu while enjoying the benefits of home life, he secretly left home and went as a sadhu to Tiruvannamalai. He never left there again. He remained for more than fifty years as Dakshinamurti, teaching the path of Self-enquiry to all who came, from India and abroad, from East and West. An Ashram grew up around him. His name of Venkataraman was shortened to Ramana, and he was also called the Maharshi, that is the Maha Rishi or Great Sage, a title traditionally given to one who inaugurates a new spiritual path. However, his devotees mostly spoke of him as Bhagavan. In speaking to him also they addressed him in the third person as Bhagavan. Self-realization means constant conscious awareness of identity with Atma, the Absolute, the Spirit, the Self of all; it is the state which Christ expressed when he said: 'I and my Father are One.' This is a very rare thing. Such a one is habitually addressed as Bhagavan, which is a name for God.

On Bhagavan's first arrival at Tiruvannamalai there was no question of disciples or teaching. He discarded even apparent interest in the manifested world, sitting immersed in that experience of Being which is integral Knowledge and ineffable Bliss, beyond life and death. Whether the body continued to live was indifferent to him, and he made no effort to sustain it. Others sustained it by bringing him daily the cup of food that was needed for its nourishment; and when he began to return gradually to a participation in the activities of life it was for the spiritual sustenance of those who had gathered around him.

The same applies also to his study of philosophy. He did not need the mind's confirmation of the resplendent Reality in which he was established, only his followers required explanations. It began with Palaniswami, a Malayali attendant who had access to books of spiritual philosophy only in Tamil. He had great difficulty in reading

---

[1] 'To view Chidambaram, to be born in Tiruvarur, to die in Benares, or merely to think of Arunachala is to be assured of Liberation.' This couplet is commonly known in the Brahmin households of South India.

[2] *Alternatively:* I realized that It meant Absolute Stillness.

Tamil, so the Maharshi read the books for him and expounded their essential meaning. Similarly he read other books for other devotees and became erudite without seeking or valuing erudition.

There was no change or development in his philosophy during the half century and more of his teaching. There could be none, since he had not worked out any philosophy but merely recognized the expositions of transcendental Truth in theory, myth, and symbol when he read them. What he taught was the ultimate doctrine of Non-duality or Advaita in which all other doctrines are finally absorbed: that Being is One and is manifested in the universe and in all creatures without ever changing from its eternal, unmanifest Self, much as, in a dream, the mind creates all the people and events a man sees without losing anything by their creation or gaining anything by their re-absorption, without ceasing to be itself.

Some found this hard to believe, taking it to imply that the world is unreal, but the Maharshi explained to them that the world is only unreal as world, that is to say as a separate, self-subsistent thing, but is real as a manifestation of the Self, just as the events one sees on a cinema screen are unreal as actual life but real as a shadow-show. Some feared that it denied the existence of a Personal God to whom they could pray, but it transcends this doctrine without denying it, for ultimately the worshipper is absorbed back into Union with the Worshipped. The man who prays, the prayer, and the God to whom he prays all have reality only as manifestations of the Self.

Just as the Maharshi realized the Self with no previous theoretical instruction, so he attached little importance to theory in training his disciples. The theory expounded in the following works is all turned to the practical purpose of helping the reader towards Self-knowledge—by which is not meant any psychological study but knowing and being the Self which exists behind the ego or mind. Questions that were asked for mere gratification of curiosity he would brush aside. If asked about the posthumous state of man he might answer: 'Why do you want to know what you will be when you die before you know what you are now? First find out what you are now.' Thus he was turning the questioner from mental curiosity to the spiritual quest. Similarly he would parry questions about *samadhi* or about the state of the *Jnani* (the Self-realized man): 'Why do you want to know about the *Jnani* before you know about yourself?

First find out who you are.' But when questions bore upon the task of self-discovery he had enormous patience in explaining.

The method of enquiry into oneself that he taught goes beyond philosophy and beyond psychology, for it is not the qualities of the ego that are sought but the Self standing resplendent without qualities when the ego ceases to function. What the mind has to do is not to suggest a reply, but to remain quiet so that the true reply can arise. 'It is not right to make an incantation of "Who am I?" Put the question only once and then concentrate on finding the source of the ego and preventing the occurrence of thoughts.' 'Finding the source of the ego' implies concentration on the spiritual centre in the body, the heart on the right side, as explained by the Maharshi. And, so concentrating, 'to prevent the occurrence of thoughts'. 'Suggestive replies to the enquiry, such as "I am Siva", are not to be given to the mind during meditation. The true answer will come of itself. No answer the ego can give can be right. These affirmations or autosuggestions may be of help to those who follow other methods but not in this method of enquiry. If you keep on asking the reply will come.' The reply comes as a current of awareness in the heart, fitful at first and only achieved by intense effort, but gradually increasing in power and constancy, becoming more spontaneous, acting as a check on thoughts and actions, undermining the ego, until finally the ego disappears and the certitude of pure Consciousness remains.

As taught by the Maharshi, Self-enquiry embraces *karma-marga* as well as *jnana-marga*, the path of action as well as that of Knowledge, for it is to be used not only as a meditation but in the events of life, assailing the manifestations of egoism by asking to whom is good or bad fortune, triumph or disaster. In this way, the circumstances of life, far from being an obstacle to *sadhana*, are made an instrument of *sadhana*. Therefore those who asked whether they should renounce the life of the world were always discouraged from doing so. Instead they were enjoined to perform their duties in life without self-interest.

It embraces the path of love and devotion also. The Maharshi said: 'There are two ways: either ask yourself, "Who am I?" or submit.' On another occasion he said: 'Submit to me and I will strike down the mind.' There were many who followed, through love, this path of submission to him. It led to the same goal. He said: 'God, Guru, and Self are not really different but the same.' Those who followed the path of Self-enquiry were seeking the Self inwardly, whereas those who strove through love were submitting to the Guru manifested outwardly. But the two were the same. That is more than ever clear to his devotees now that the Maharshi has left the body and become the Inner Guru in the heart of each one of them.

It was thus a new and integral path that the Maharshi opened to those who turn to him. The ancient path of Self-enquiry was pure *jnana-marga* to be followed in silent meditation by the hermit and had, moreover, been considered by the Sages unsuited to this *kali-yuga*, this spiritually dark age in which we live. What Bhagavan did was not so much to restore the old path as to create a new one adapted to the conditions of our age, a path that can be followed in city or household no less than in forest or hermitage, with a period of meditation each day and constant remembering throughout the day's activities, with or without the support of outer observances.

The Maharshi wrote very little. He taught mainly through the tremendous power of Spiritual Silence. That did not mean that he was unwilling to answer questions when asked. So long as he felt that they were asked with a sincere motive and not out of idle curiosity, he answered fully whether in speech or writing. However, it was the silent influence upon the heart that was the essential teaching.

Nearly everything that he wrote was in response to some request, to meet the specific needs of some devotee, and therefore a short note is given at the beginning of the various items explaining their genesis. This is for the interest of the reader, but the particular need that evoked them does not in any way impair the universality of their scope.

It is to be noted that the verse items are not arranged in chronological order. They were arranged in order by Bhagavan himself, for a devotee who kept a private collection of them, and therefore the same order has been retained here.

A word about the translation. The Ashram has translations of the various works, a number of translations of some of them; and all that the present editor has done is to select one and improve the English of it where necessary, without changing the meaning.

PART ONE

Original Works

I

Self-Enquiry

SELF-ENQUIRY is the first work the Maharshi ever wrote. It was written about 1901, that is when he was a young man of about twenty-two. He was already a *Jnani* or Sage in perfect realization of the Self, in the resplendent bliss of Divine Knowledge. At that time he was living in Virupaksha cave on the hill of Aruna-chala. A number of disciples had already gathered round him. Although he had not actually taken a vow of silence, he seldom spoke, and to this we owe his writing out this book of instructions when one of his disciples, Gambhiram Seshayya, asked for guidance.

There is no youthfulness or immaturity in the work. The Master wrote with the authority of full spiritual knowledge, just as in his later years. Like all his expositions, verbal as well as written, this is concerned with practical questions of the path to Realization of the Self, never with barren theory. However, it does differ from later expositions in one important respect: that is that it describes not only the path of Self-enquiry but others also, meditation on one's identity with the Self and a yogic path based on breath-control. He himself prescribed only Self-enquiry or submission to the Guru. He would say: 'There are two ways: ask yourself "Who am I?" or submit.'

Why did he include the mention of less direct and more elaborate methods in this first exposition? The obvious contingent reason is that the disciple for whom it was written had been reading books about these various methods and asked questions about them. Perhaps also, in a wider sense, it is appropriate that there should first be a general exposition of various methods before the lifelong instruction in that which he prescribed. Certainly the other methods, although described, are scarcely recommended. In deprecation of

17

meditation on one's identity with the Self, he says on page 18: 'this is still a thought, but one which is necessary to those minds which are addicted to much thinking.' He definitely says on page 26 that the most competent seekers take the path of Self-enquiry, that those who are less competent meditate on identity, while those on a still lower level practise breath-control. Moreover, after giving a brief outline of the yogic path based on breath-control he says, on page 22, that anyone who wants to learn more about it must go to a practising yogi who gives instruction in this way—a clear indication that he himself did not.

The breath-control that is described is, of course, no mere physical exercise. It is the spiritual significance of the exercise that makes it an elaborate science. 'Science' is, indeed, the right word for it, for it is a traditional Indian science of self-purification. This makes it abstruse for the Western reader who has no previous grounding in it, especially as, like all sciences, it has its technical vocabulary which does not permit of adequate translation without lengthy notes. One has to remember that in writing this exposition the Maharshi knew that he could count on a technical knowledge of the science in question in the person for whom he wrote. The consolation for Western readers is to remember that he neither recommended nor prescribed this path and in his later works scarcely mentioned it. It is not necessary for them to learn its technicalities.

ENQUIRY INTO THE SELF

In this chapter is given clearly the path of
enquiry into the Self, or 'Who Am I?'

Is not the sense of 'I' natural to all beings, expressed in all their feelings as 'I came', 'I went', 'I did', or 'I was'? On questioning what this is, we find that the body is identified with 'I', because movements and similar functions pertain to the body. Can the body then be this 'I-consciousness'? It was not there before birth, it is composed of the five elements, it is absent[1] in sleep, and it (eventually) becomes a

[1] i.e. from our awareness.

corpse. No, it cannot be. This sense of 'I', which arises in the body for the time being, is otherwise called the ego, ignorance, illusion, impurity, or individual self. The purpose of all the scriptures is this enquiry (into the Self). It is declared in them that the annihilation of the ego-sense is Liberation. How then can one remain indifferent to this teaching? Can the body, which is insentient as a piece of wood, shine and function as 'I'? No. Therefore, lay aside this insentient body as though it were truly a corpse. Do not even murmur 'I', but enquire keenly within what it is that now shines within the heart as 'I'. Underlying the unceasing flow of varied thoughts, there arises the continuous, unbroken awareness, silent and spontaneous, as 'I-I' in the Heart. If one catches hold of it and remains still, it will completely annihilate the sense of 'I' in the body, and will itself disappear as a fire of burning camphor. Sages and scriptures proclaim this to be Liberation.

The veil of ignorance can never completely hide the individual self. How can it? Even the ignorant do not fail to speak of the 'I'. It only hides the Reality, 'I-am-the-Self', or 'I am pure Consciousness', and confounds the 'I' with the body.

The Self is self-effulgent. One need give it no mental picture, anyway. The thought that imagines it is itself bondage, because the Self is the Effulgence transcending darkness and light; one should not think of it with the mind. Such imagination will end in bondage, whereas the Self spontaneously shines as the Absolute. This enquiry into the Self in devotional meditation evolves into the state of absorption of the mind into the Self and leads to Liberation and unqualified Bliss. The great Sages have declared that only by the help of this devotional enquiry into the Self can Liberation be attained. Because the ego in the form of the 'I-thought' is the root of the tree of illusion, its destruction fells illusion, even as a tree is felled by the cutting of its roots. This easy method of annihilating the ego is alone worthy to be called *bhakti* (devotion), *Jnana* (Knowledge), *yoga* (union), or *dhyana* (meditation).

In the 'I-am-the-body' consciousness, the three bodies[1] composed of the five sheaths[2] are contained. If that mode of consciousness is removed all else drops off of its own accord; all other bodies

---

[1] i.e. the physical, subtle, and causal—of the waking, dream, and sleep states respectively.
[2] i.e. the gross, sensory, mental, intellectual, and blissful.

depend on it. There is no need to eliminate them separately because the scriptures declare that thought alone is bondage. It is their final injunction that the best method is to surrender the mind in the form of the 'I'-thought to Him (the Self) and, keeping quite still, not forget Him.

THE NATURE OF THE MIND

*In this chapter are described briefly the nature
of the mind, its states and location.*

According to the Hindu scriptures there exists an entity known as the 'mind', which is derived from the subtle essence of the food consumed; which flourishes as love, hatred, lust, anger, and so on; which is the totality of mentality, intellect, desire, and ego; which, although it has such diverse functions, bears the generic name 'mind', which is objectified as the insentient objects cognized by us; which, though itself insentient, appears to be sentient, being associated with Consciousness, just as a piece of red-hot iron appears to be fire; in which the principle of differentiation is inherent; which is transient and is possessed of parts capable of being moulded into any shape like lac, gold, or wax; which is the basis of all root-principles (*tattvas*); which is located in the Heart like sight in the eye and hearing in the ear; which gives its character to the individual self and which, on thinking of the object already associated with the consciousness reflected on the brain, assumes a thought-form; which is in contact with that object through the five senses operated by the brain, which appropriates such cognizance to itself with the feeling 'I am cognizant of such and such', enjoys the object and is finally satisfied.

To think whether a certain thing may be eaten is a thought-form of the mind. 'It is good. It is not good. It can be eaten. It cannot be eaten': discriminating notions like these constitute the discriminative intellect. Because the mind alone constitutes the root-principle manifesting as the three entities of ego, God, and world, its absorption and dissolution in the Self is the final emancipation known as *kaivalya*, which is the same as Brahman.

The senses, being located externally as aids for the cognition of objects, are exterior; the mind, being internal, is the inner sense. 'Within' and 'without' are relative to the body; they have no significance in the Absolute. For the purpose of showing the whole objective world to be within, and not without, the scriptures have described the cosmos as being shaped like the lotus of the Heart. But that is not other than the Self. Just as the goldsmith's wax ball, although hiding minute specks of gold, still looks like a simple lump of wax, so too all the individuals merged in dark ignorance (*avidya*), or the universal veiling (*Maya*), are only aware of nescience in their sleep. In deep sleep the physical and subtle bodies, though entering in the dark veiling, still lie merged in the Self. From ignorance sprang the ego—the subtle body. The mind must be transformed into the Self.

Mind is, in reality, only consciousness, because it is pure and transparent by nature: in that pure state, however, it cannot be called mind. The wrong identification of one thing with another[1] is the work of the contaminated mind. That is to say, the pure, uncontaminated mind, being absolute Consciousness, on becoming oblivious of its primary nature, is overpowered by the quality of darkness (*tamas*) and manifests as the physical world. Similarly, overpowered by activity (*rajas*), it identifies itself with the body and, appearing in the manifested world as 'I', mistakes this ego for the reality. Thus, swayed by love and hatred, it performs good and bad actions, and is, as the result, caught up in the cycle of births and deaths. It is the experience of everyone that in deep sleep and in a faint he has no awareness of his own Self or of objectivity. Later the experience 'I woke up from sleep', 'I regained consciousness', is the distinctive knowledge born of the natural state. This distinctive knowledge is called *vijnana*. It shines not by itself but by always adhering either to the Self or the non-Self. When it inheres in the Self, it is called true Knowledge; it is awareness of the mental mode in the Self, or perpetual awareness; and when this distinctive knowledge combines with the non-Self, it is called ignorance. The state in which it inheres in the Self and shines as the Self is termed *aham*

---

[1] i.e. the mistaken view that attributes the Reality of the Self to the material world as existing by itself independent of the conscious principle. This is due to the false identification of the Self with the physical body, as a result of which the ignorant person assumes that what is outside and independent of the physical body is also outside and independent of the conscious principle.

spurana or the pulsation of the Self. This is not something apart from the Self; it is a sign of the forthcoming realization of the Self. However, this is not the state of Primal Being. The source in which this pulsation is revealed is called *prajnana* (Consciousness). It is this source that Vedanta proclaims as *prajnana ghana*. The Vivekachuda-mani of Shankaracharya describes this Eternal State as follows: 'In the sheath of intelligence shines eternally *Atman*, the self-effulgent witness of all. Making that thy Goal, which is quite different from the unreal, enjoy it by experience, through unbroken thought-current as thy own Self.'

THE THREE STATES

The ever luminous Self is one and universal. Notwithstanding the individual's experience of the three states—waking, dream, and deep sleep—the Self remains pure and changeless. It is not limited by the three bodies, physical, mental, and causal; and It transcends the triple relation of seer, sight, and seen. The diagram on the next page will be found helpful in understanding the changeless state of the Self, transcending the illusory manifestations referred to above.

The sketch illustrates how the luminous Consciousness of the Self, shining by Itself, functions as the causal body (7) in the inner chamber surrounded by walls of ignorance (*avidya*) (4) and led by the door of sleep (2), which is moved by the vital forces, due to the lapse of time and according to destiny, through the doorway (3) against the interposed mirror of the ego (5). It passes with the light reflected therefrom into the middle chamber of the dream state (8); later is projected into the open courtyard of wakefulness (9) through the passage of the five senses or windows (6). When the door of sleep (2) is shut by the force of mind (i.e. the vital forces) due to the lapse of time and according to destiny, it retires from the wakeful and dream states into deep sleep and remains merely as itself without the ego-sense. The sketch also illustrates the serene existence of the Self as different from the ego and from the three states of sleep, dream, and wakefulness.

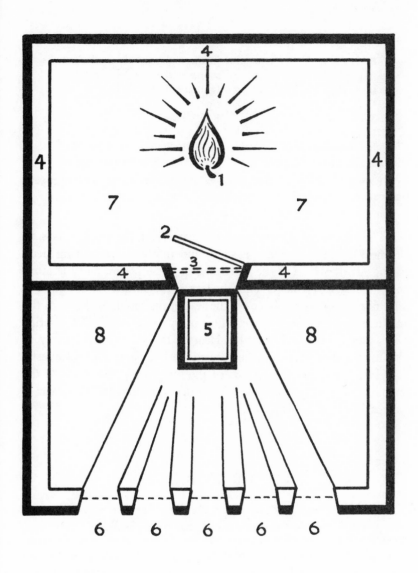

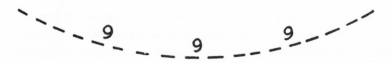

1. Flame ... ... represents the Self.
2. Door ... ... ,, Sleep.

3. Doorway ...	... represents	Intellectual principle (*mahat*) as the source of the ego (*ahankar*).
4. Inner wall	...	,,	Ignorance (*avidya*).
5. Crystal mirror	...	,,	Ego.
6. Windows	...	,,	Five senses.
7. Inner chamber	...	,,	Causal body during sleep.
8. Middle chamber	...	,,	Subtle body in dream state.
9. Open court-yard	...	,,	Physical body in waking state.

The inner and the middle chambers together with the open court-yard represent the individual.

The individual self resides in the eye during the waking state, in the neck[1] during the dream state, and in the Heart during deep sleep; but the Heart is the chief among these places, and therefore the individual self never entirely leaves the Heart. Although it is specifically said that the neck is the seat of the mind, the brain of the intellect, and the Heart or the whole body of the ego, still the scriptures state conclusively that the Heart is the seat of that totality of the inner senses[2] which is called the mind. The Sages, having investigated all the different versions of the scriptures, briefly stated the whole truth that it is the experience of everyone that the Heart is primarily the seat of the 'I'.

THE WORLD

In this chapter it is shown that the world has no reality of its own and does not exist apart from the Self.

Creation: The main purpose of the scriptures is to expose the illusory nature of the world and to reveal the Supreme Spirit as the only Reality. They have built up the theory of creation with this sole end in view. They even go into detail and entertain the lowest order of seekers with the narration of the successive appearance of the Spirit, of the disequilibrium[3] of reflected consciousness, of the fundamentals

---

[1] At the back of the neck in the *medulla oblongata*.

[2] *Antahkarana*, in the original, meaning the mind, intellect, and ego collectively.

[3] *Prakriti*, in the original, meaning the disturbance of the balance of the three qualities in Nature, viz. harmony, activity, and darkness, which precede the manifestation of primordial matter.

of elements, of the world, of the body, of life, and so on. But for the higher order of seekers the scriptures would say, in short, that the whole world appears like a panorama in a dream with an apparent objectivity and independent existence due to ignorance of the Self and consequent obsession with obtrusive thoughts. They seek to show the world as an illusion in order to reveal the Truth. Those who have realized the Self by direct and immediate experience clearly perceive beyond all doubt that the phenomenal world as an objective, independent reality is wholly non-existent.

DISCRIMINATION BETWEEN THE SEER AND THE SEEN

Object seen: insentient	*The seer: sentient*
The body, a pot, etc.	the eye
The eye	the optic nerve-centre in the brain
The optic nerve-centre	the mind
The mind	the individual self or ego
The individual self	pure Consciousness.

Since the Self, which is pure Consciousness, cognizes everything, as stated in the classification above, It is the ultimate Seer. All the rest: ego, mind, etc., are merely its objects. The subject in one line becomes the object in the next; so each one of them except the Self or pure Consciousness is a merely externalized object and cannot be the true Seer. Since the Self cannot be objectified, not being cognized by anything else, and since the Self is the Seer seeing all else, the subject-object relation and the apparent subjectivity of the Self exist only on the plane of relativity and vanish in the Absolute. There is in truth no other than the Self, which is neither the seer nor the seen, and is not involved as subject or object.

THE EGO (JIVA)

In this chapter, the Self (Atma) itself is said to be the ego (Jiva) and the nature of the ego is explained.

The mind is nothing else than the 'I'-thought. The mind and the ego are one and the same. Intellect, will, ego, and individuality are collectively the same mind. It is like a man being variously described according to his different activities. The individual is nothing else than the ego, which, again, is only the mind. Simultaneously with the rise of the ego the mind appears, associated with the reflected nature of the Self, like the red-hot iron in the example.[1] How is the fire in the red-hot iron to be understood? As being one with it? Since the individual is nothing else than the ego and is inseparable from the Self, as the fire and the red-hot iron are, there is no other self to act as witness of the individual than the individual himself functioning as the ego, which after all is only the mind associated with reflected Consciousness. The very same Self not only shines unaffected in the Heart, like the fire in the iron,[2] but is also infinite like space. It is self-luminous in the Heart as pure Consciousness, as the One without a second and, manifesting universally as the same in all individuals, it is known as the Supreme Spirit. 'Heart' is merely another name for the Supreme Spirit, because He is in all Hearts.

Thus the red-hot iron is the individual, the fiery heat is the witnessing Self, the iron is the ego. The pure fire is the all-immanent and all-knowing Supreme Spirit.

THE SUPREME BEING IS THE SELF

In this chapter it is shown that the form of the Self is the form of God and He is in the form of 'I-I'.

The universal principle underlying the correspondence between the ideas 'within' and the objects 'without' is the true significance of the term 'mind'. Therefore, the body and the world which appear as external to oneself are only mental reflections. It is only the Heart that manifests in all these forms. In the Core of the all-comprehensive Heart, that is, in the expanse of the pure mind, there is the

---

[1] It is a commonly used example in India that, just as red-hot iron partakes of the nature of fire through contact with it, so the mind or ego partakes of the nature of Consciousness through contact with the Self.

[2] Just as the fire in the red-hot iron is unaffected by the hammer-blows, which only change the shape of the metal, so the vicissitudes of life, pleasure and pain, affect only the ego, the Self ever remaining pure and undefiled.

self-luminous 'I' always shining. Because It is manifest in everybody, it is also called the Omniscient Witness, or the Fourth State.[1]

The Infinite Expanse is the Reality known as the Supreme Spirit or the Self, which shines without egoism as the Consciousness within the 'I', as the One in all individuals. What is beyond the Fourth State is only this. Let it be meditated on, the Expanse of Absolute Consciousness which shines, all-pervading, within and without the illumination of the Fourth State, like space which simultaneously pervades the inmost blue core of a luminous flame and the infinite space beyond. The true State is that which shines all over, as space includes and extends beyond the flame. No heed should be paid to the light. Enough to know that the Real is the State free from ego. That every one points to the chest when referring to himself by gesture is sufficient proof that the Absolute resides as the Self in the Heart. The Rishi Vasishtha also says that searching for the Self outside oneself, oblivious of its constantly shining as 'I-I' within the Heart, is like throwing away an invaluable celestial gem for a sparkling pebble. Vedantists[2] consider it a sacrilege to regard the One Creating, Sustaining, and Absorbing Supreme Self as the separate gods, Ganapathi, Brahman, Vishnu, Rudra, Maheswara, and Sadasiva.[3]

KNOWLEDGE OF THE SUPREME SELF

In this chapter is described the method of realizing the Self.

When the mind in the form of the ego, which takes the body for the Self and strays outwards, is curbed within the Heart, the sense of 'I' in the body relinquished, and enquiry made with a still mind as to who it is that dwells in the body, a subtle illumination will be experienced as 'I-I', which is no other than the Absolute, the Self, seated in the lotus of the Heart, in the city of the body, the tabernacle of

[1] Waking is the first state, dreaming is the second, and deep sleep is the third. Since pure Consciousness subsists during all the three states and also transcends them, it cannot strictly be classified along with the other three states, though it is technically called the Fourth State.

[2] The adherents of the Hindu doctrine which postulates One Supreme Reality and dismisses the names and forms of all else as illusion.

[3] Ganapati is the son of Rudra, Brahma is the God of Creation, Vishnu of Preservation, Rudra or Siva of Destruction, Maheswara of universal veiling, Sadasiva is the Deity whose bestowal of Grace removes the veiling.

God. Then one should remain still, with the conviction that the Self shines as everything yet nothing, within, without, and everywhere, and is also the transcendental Being. This is known as meditation on the Truth conveyed by the dictum 'Sivoham', 'I am Siva', and is also called the Fourth State.

That which is even beyond this subtle experience is God, variously termed the State beyond the Fourth, the Omnipresent, Supreme Being which shines as the Core of the Divine Flame within, and described as manifesting in concentration and meditation, the Sixth and Seventh steps of the Eightfold Yoga, the Expanse of the Heart, pure Consciousness, the Absolute shining in the mind's sky, Bliss, the Self, and Wisdom. By long, continuous, and steady practice of this meditation on the Self as 'I am the Supreme', the veil of ignorance in the Heart and all the resultant obstructions will be removed, and perfect Wisdom will result. Knowing in this manner the Real indwelling in the cavity of the Heart, in the tabernacle of the body, is indeed realizing the Absolute, which is inherent in all, because the Heart comprises all that exists. This is confirmed by the scriptural text, 'The Sage abides blissful in the city of nine gates which is the body', and 'The body is the temple, the individual self is the Absolute. If He is worshipped as "The Supreme I am", Liberation will result; the Spirit which bears the body in the form of five sheaths is the cavity; the cavity is only the Heart, the transcendental Being residing therein is the Lord of the Cave.' This method of realizing the Absolute is known as *dahara vidya* or Intuitive Knowledge of the Heart. What more is there to say? One should realize It by direct, immediate experience.

WORSHIP IS ONLY SELF-ENQUIRY

*In this chapter it is said that perennial awareness of the Self
is real worship and penance* (tapas).

The purpose of worshipping the Impersonal Supreme Being is the incessant remembrance of the truth that you are Brahman, because the meditation 'I am Brahman' comprises sacrifice, gifts, penance, ritual, prayer, yoga, and worship. The only way to overcome obstructions to your meditation is to forbid the mind to dwell on them and to introvert it into the Self and there witness unconcernedly all that happens; there is no other method. Do not even for a moment lose sight of the Self. Fixing the mind on the Self or the 'I' abiding in the Heart is the perfection of yoga, meditation, wisdom, devotion, and worship. Since the Supreme Being abides as the Self, constant surrender of the mind by absorption in the Self is said to comprise all forms of worship. Mind controlled, all else is controlled. The mind is itself the life-current; the ignorant say that in form it looks like a coiled serpent.[1] The six subtle centres[2] (*chakras*) are merely mental pictures and are meant for beginners in yoga. We project ourselves into the idols and worship them, because we do not understand true inward worship. Knowledge of the Self, which knows all, is Knowledge in perfection.

Distracted as we are by various thoughts, if we would continually contemplate the Self, which is Itself God, this single thought would in due course replace all distraction and would itself ultimately vanish; the pure Consciousness that alone finally remains is God. This is Liberation. Never to be heedless of one's own all-perfect, pure Self is the acme of yoga, wisdom, and all other forms of spiritual practice. Even though the mind wanders restlessly, involved in external matters, and so is forgetful of its own Self, one should remain alert and remember: 'The body is not I. Who am I?' Enquire in this way, turning the mind backward to its primal state. The enquiry 'Who am I?' is the only method of putting an end to all misery and ushering in supreme Beatitude. Whatever may be said and however phrased, this is the whole truth in a nutshell.

---

[1] *Kundalini* in the original, usually meaning a mysterious dynamic force dormant at the base of the spine, whose arousal is said to confer first thaumaturgic powers and then spiritual Illumination.
[2] These are said to be centres in the subtle body along the spine from the sacral region to the top of the head: the life-current in its upward passage forces its way into them and in doing so confers thaumaturgic and other powers.

LIBERATION

This chapter teaches that Liberation can indeed be obtained by constant and prolonged meditation on the Self in the form of 'Sivoham' (I am Siva) which means 'I am Atman'. The characteristics of Jivanmukti (Liberation in this life) and Videhamukti (Liberation after death) are described.

Because the individual self, which is nothing but the mind, has lost the knowledge of its identity with the real Self, and has enmeshed itself in bondage, its search for the Self, its own eternal primal nature, resembles that of the shepherd searching for a lamb which all the time he bears on his own shoulders.

However, the Self-oblivious ego, even when once made aware of the Self, does not get Liberation, that is Self-Realization, on account of the obstruction of accumulated mental tendencies. It frequently confuses the body with the Self, forgetting that it is itself in truth the Self. Long-cultivated tendencies can indeed be eradicated by long-continued meditation: 'I am not the body, the senses, the mind, etc., I am the Self.' Therefore, the ego, that is, the mind, which is nothing but a bundle of tendencies, and which confuses the body with 'I', should be subdued, and thus should the supreme liberated State known as Self-realization be reached after prolonged devotional worship of the divine Self, which is the very Being of all the gods. This self-investigation annihilates the mind, and itself gets destroyed eventually, just as a stick used to stir the funeral pyre is itself finally burnt. This is the state of Liberation. Self, Wisdom, Knowledge, Consciousness, the Absolute, and God denote the same thing.

Can a man become a high officer by merely once seeing such an officer? He may become one if he strives and equips himself for the position. Similarly, can the ego, which is in bondage as the mind, become the divine Self, simply because it has once glimpsed that it is the Self? Is this not impossible without the destruction of the mind? Can a beggar become a king by merely visiting a king and declaring himself one? Similarly, unless the bond of the mind is cut asunder by prolonged and unbroken meditation, 'I am the Self, the Absolute,' it is impossible to attain the transcendental State of Bliss, which is identical with the annihilation of the mind. 'The Self is the Absolute and the Absolute is the Self. The Self is the Absolute alone. That which is covered with husk is paddy, and when husked becomes rice. So also, when under bondage of action one is the individual self, and when the veil is removed one shines as the Absolute.' Thus proclaim the scriptures, which further declare: 'The mind should be drawn within and restrained in the Heart until the ego-sense, which sprouts as the ignorant mind, is therein destroyed. This is wisdom and meditation as well; all else is mere lecturing and pedantry;' and in consonance with this final word, one should fix the mind on Him, be aware of Him and realize Him by every possible endeavour.

Just as a Brahmin actor does not forget that he is a Brahmin, whatever part he may be acting, so also a man should not confuse himself with his body, but should have a firm awareness of his being the Self, whatever his activity may be. This awareness will manifest as the mind gets absorbed in its own primal State. Such absorption leads to Bliss Supreme when the Self reveals itself spontaneously. Then one will not be affected by pleasure and pain, which result from contact with external objects. Everything will be perceived without attachment, as in a dream. Such thoughts as 'Is this good or that?', 'Is this to be done or that?' should not be allowed to arise. Immediately a thought arises, it should be annihilated at its source. If entertained even for a little while, it will hurl one down headlong like a treacherous friend. Can the mind which is fixed in its original State possess an ego-sense, or have any problem to solve? Do not such thoughts themselves constitute bondage? Hence when such thoughts arise due to past tendencies, not only should the mind be curbed and turned back to its true State, but also it should be made to remain unconcerned and indifferent to external happenings. Is it not due to Self-forgetfulness that such thoughts arise and cause more and more misery? Though the discriminating thought, 'I am not the doer; all actions are merely the reactions of the body, senses and mind', is an aid for turning back the mind to its primal state, nevertheless it is still a thought, but one which is necessary for those minds which are addicted to much thinking. On the other hand, can the mind, fixed unswervingly in the divine Self and remaining unaffected even while engaged in activities, give in to such thoughts as 'I am the body, I am engaged in work', or again to the discriminating thought, 'I am not the doer, these actions are merely reactions of the body, senses and mind'? Gradually one should, by all possible means, try always to be aware of the Self. Everything is achieved if one succeeds in this. Let not the mind be diverted to any other object. One should abide in the Self without the sense of being the doer, even when engaged in work born of destiny, like a mad-man. Have not many devotees achieved much with a detached atti-tude and firm devotion of this nature?

Because the quality of purity (*sattva*) is the real nature of the mind, clearness like that of the unclouded sky is the characteristic of the mind-expanse. Being stirred up by the quality of activity (*rajas*) the mind becomes restless and, influenced by darkness (*tamas*), manifests as the physical world. The mind thus becoming restless on the one hand and appearing as solid matter on the other, the Real is not discerned. Just as fine silk threads cannot be woven with the use of a heavy iron shuttle, or the delicate shades of a work of art be distinguished in the light of a lamp flickering in the wind, so is Realization of Truth impossible with the mind rendered gross by darkness (*tamas*) and restless by activity (*rajas*). Because Truth is exceedingly subtle and serene, Mind will be cleared of its impuri-ties only by a desireless performance of duties during several births, getting a worthy Master, learning from him and incessantly practis-ing meditation on the Supreme. The transformation of the mind into the world of inert matter due to the quality of darkness (*tamas*) and its restlessness due to the quality of activity (*rajas*) will cease. Then the mind regains its subtlety and composure. The Bliss of the Self can manifest only in a mind rendered subtle and steady by assiduous meditation. He who experiences that Bliss is liberated even while still alive.

When the mind is divested of the qualities of darkness and activity by constant meditation, the Bliss of the Self will clearly manifest within the subtle mind. Yogis gain omniscience by means of such mind-expanse. He alone who has achieved such subtlety of mind and has gained Realization of the Self is Liberated while still alive. The same state has been described in Rama Gita[1] as the

---

[1] Hindu sacred book handed down from antiquity.

Brahman beyond attributes, the one universal undifferentiated Spirit. He who has attained the unbroken eternal State beyond even that, transcending mind and speech, is called *videhamukta*; that is, when even the aforesaid subtle mind is destroyed, the experience of Bliss as such also ceases. He is drowned and dissolved in the fathomless Ocean of Bliss and is unaware of anything apart. This is *videhamukti*. There is nothing beyond it. It is the end of all.

As one continues to abide as the Self, the experience 'I am the Supreme Spirit' grows and becomes natural; the restlessness of the mind and the thought of the world in due course become extinct. Because experience is not possible without the mind, Realization takes place with the subtle mind. Since *videhamukti* connotes the entire dissolution of even the subtle mind, this State is beyond experience. It is the transcendental State. 'I am not the body. I am the pure Spirit' is the clear and indubitable experience of the *jivanmukta*, that is one who is liberated while yet alive. Nevertheless, if the mind is not totally destroyed, there is the possibility of his becoming apparently unhappy in his incidental association with objects, as ordained by his destiny.[1] He may also appear to the onlooker as not having realized the unbroken eternal Bliss, because his mind seems to be agitated. However, the Bliss of Liberation in life is possible only to the mind made subtle and serene by long continued meditation.

THE EIGHTFOLD PATH OF YOGA

In this chapter is described the path of yoga for obtaining Self-Realization, getting control of the mind through control of breath.

For achieving devotion in the form of meditation described in the previous chapter, steps like *yama* and *niyama* (the first two stages in *ashtanga* or eightfold yoga, explained below) are prescribed. These have two forms, one of the nature of yoga and the other of *jnana*.

---

[1] *Prarabdha*, in the original, meaning the accumulated fruits of actions of former lives which are now being reaped.

Control over breath is yoga. Elimination of the mind is *jnana*. Which of these comes more easily to the aspirant depends on his inherent tendencies and maturity. Both lead to the same result since by control of breath the mind gets controlled, and by elimination of the mind the breath gets controlled. The object of both these methods is the subsidence and elimination of the mind.

Yama (moral self-control which is the necessary preliminary to the yogic path; in detail: abstention from lying, killing, theft, lust, and covetousness), *niyama* (disciplinary observances), *pratyahara* (withdrawal of the senses from external objects), *dharana* (concentrated attention), *dhyana* (steady uninterrupted contemplation), *samadhi* (identification of oneself with the Atman). These eight are the elements of yoga. Of these breath-control, which forms part of *niyama*, consists of exhalation, inhalation and retention. While in all the sastras it is said that exhalation and inhalation should be equal and retention twice their length, in Rajayoga, retention of breath is four times as long as inhalation and twice as long as exhalation. The breath-control of the Rajayoga path is superior to other kinds. If this breath-control is practised according to one's capacity, without strain but regularly, the body gets fatigued in a way but becomes still and the desire to be in a state of Bliss gradually arises in the mind. Then *pratyahara* must be attempted. This unifies the mind and makes it one-pointed, so that it does not run after the external objects of name and form. Since the mind that has till now run after externals can rarely withdraw and steady itself, efforts are made to unify and steady it by holding it to a particular aim by the following means: *pranava japa* (the incantation of Om) and other incantations made mentally; fixing the attention between the eyebrows; concentrating on the tip of the nose; hearing the sounds arising within the ears alternately, i.e. striving to hear the sound in the left ear with the right ear and *vice versa*. *Dharana* (concentrated attention) must then be attempted. This means fixing the mind on a centre fit for meditation. The heart and *brahmarandhra* (fontanelle or aperture in the crown of the head) are recommended as fit spots for *dharana*. The mind is fixed on either of these spots while conceiving of one's personal deity in the form of a flame of light shining there. If one fixes one's attention on the heart it is the eight-petalled lotus; if on the *brahmarandhra* it is also the eight-petalled lotus, though said to consist of *sahasradala* (a thousand petals) or 125 small petals. Thus concentrating, one must meditate that one is not a separate being from one's deity and that that flame of light is the form of one's Atma (Spirit or Self). In other words, it is meditation on 'I am He'. The scripture says that the all-pervasive Brahman itself is shining in the heart as 'I, I', the witness of the intellect. If one asks 'Who am I?' then He (the Deity or the Atma) will be found shining (throbbing) as 'I, I' in the lotus of the heart. Practising this is also meditation and is much better than the 'I am He' meditation. A man can practise whatever comes easy to him. By practice of this kind of meditation, one becomes unaware of oneself and what one is doing and one's mind gets absorbed in the Self. The subtle state in which even the pulsation subsides is the state of *samadhi*. Only, one must guard against sleep in this state. Then it will confer Supreme Bliss. If anyone practises this daily and regularly, God will bless him on the Supreme Path, on which he will attain perfect Peace. As there are elaborate treatises on the elements of *ashtanga* yoga, only as much as is necessary is written here. Anyone who desires to know more must resort to a practising yogi with experience and learn from him in detail.

Pranava is incantation of OM with three and a half beats, A, U, M, and a half beat of M. Of these A stands for the waking state, the gross body, and creation, U stands for the dream state, the subtle body, and preservation, M stands for deep sleep, the Self at rest in sleep, the causal body, and dissolution. The half sound stands for the fourth state, the true state of the I or Self. The state beyond this is the state of pure Bliss. The fourth state obtained in meditation as one's true State contains within itself A, U, M and the half beat and so is called the state in which all sound forms have subsided; it is also called silent incantation and non-dual incantation, which is the essence of all incantations. It is for obtaining this true experience of OM that in the stage of *pratyahara* silent incantation is prescribed.

'The soul attains conscious immortality through meditating upon that principle ever shining like the flame of light possessing the effulgence of lightning, residing as All-Pervading in the midst of the heart lotus with eight-petals, the size of a thumb and described variously as *kailas*, *vaikunta*, and *paramapada*.' The seeker is advised to meditate in accordance with this text. A sense of inconstancy in the Self may appear to arise and also of differentiation between the meditator and what he meditates upon. The seeker is advised to meditate upon his own Self, because that flame which is throbbing as I, I is the Self. Therefore there need be no doubting this scriptural text. Of all forms of meditation, *atma dhyana* (meditation on the Self), which has just been described, is the best. If that is achieved there is no need to attempt other forms of meditation, because all are included in it. Other forms are advised only to help achieve success in this. The form of meditation one follows will depend on one's maturity of mind. Though the various modes of meditation may appear different, yet they all converge on the same point; there is no need to doubt this. 'Knowing one's own Self is knowing God. Not knowing the nature of him who meditates but meditating on God as foreign to one's own Self is like measuring one's shadow with one's foot. You go on measuring while the shadow also goes on receding further and further.' So say the scriptures. Hence meditation on the Self is best, because the Self alone is the Supreme Self of all the gods.

THE EIGHTFOLD PATH OF KNOWLEDGE

In this chapter is described the jnanamarga (the path of Knowledge) which leads to Self-Realization through realization that the Supreme is One and Indivisible.

Detailed description of the phases of *jnana ashtanga* (the eightfold path of Knowledge) such as *yama* and *niyama* is beyond the scope of this small work. Exhalation in this path means giving up the two aspects of name and form, of body and world. Inhalation is taking in (grasping) the *sat* (being), *chit* (consciousness), *ananda* (bliss) aspects pervading names and forms. Retention of breath is retaining them, assimilating what has been taken in. *Pratyahara* is being ever on the vigil that the rejected names and forms do not intrude again into the mind. *Dharana* is retaining the mind in the heart, so that it does not wander, by holding firm to the concept already grasped, that is: 'I am the *sat chit ananda Atman*' (the Self which is Being-

Consciousness-Bliss). *Dhyana* (meditation) is steady abidance as *aham swarupa* (in one's true form) which is experienced as 'I, I' of its own accord, just as when enquiring 'Who am I?', by stilling the corpse of this body of five sheaths. For this kind of breath-control there is no need of such regulations as *asanas* (postures) etc. One may practise it in any place or time. The primary aim is to fix the mind in the Heart at the feet of the Lord shining as the Self and never to forget Him. Forgetfulness of the Self is the source of all misery. The elders say that such forgetfulness is death to the aspirant after Liberation. It may be asked if the regular breath-control of Rajayoga (a yogic path) is unnecessary. To this we reply: it is useful, but its value lasts only as long as one is practising it, whereas the breath-control of the eightfold path of Knowledge is a permanent help. The aim of both kinds of breath-control is to remember the Self and to still the mind. Therefore until the mind has subsided in the heart by means of breath-control or Self-enquiry regular yogic breath-control remains necessary; further than that there is no need for it. The *kevala kumbhaka* type of breath-control is of such nature that the breathing subsides in the Heart even without control of inhalation and exhalation. One may practise the methods of either yoga or *jnana* (knowledge) as one will.

All the scriptures aim at control of the mind, since destruction of the mind is *moksha* or Liberation. Yoga is control of the breath, while the method of *jnana* or Knowledge is to see everything as a form of truth or as Brahman the One and Indivisible. It depends on a person's latent tendencies which of these two paths will appeal to him. The path of Knowledge is like taming an unruly bull by showing it a bundle of grass, that of yoga is like taming it by beating and yoking it. So say those who know. Fully competent persons reach the Goal by controlling the mind, in the truth of Vedanta, knowing the certainty of the Self, and seeing their Self and everything as Brahman. Those who are less qualified fix the mind in the heart by means of breath-control and prolonged meditation on the Self. Those who are still less qualified reach higher stages by methods such as breath-control. Bearing this in mind, the yoga of the control of mind is classified as the eightfold path of Knowledge and of yoga. It is enough if breath-control is practised till *kevala kumbhaka* is achieved. Direct experience of *samadhi* can also be attained by devotion (*bhakti*) in the form of constant meditation (*dhyana*). *Kevala kumbhaka* with Self-enquiry, even without control of inhalation and exhalation, is an aid to this. If that becomes natural to one, it can be practised at all times except during worldly activity and there is no need to seek a special place for it. Whatever a person finds suitable may be practised. If the mind gradually subsides, it does not matter if other things come and go. In the Bhagavad Gita, Lord Krishna says that the devotee is higher than the yogi and that the means to Liberation is *bhakti* (devotion) in the form of inherence in the Self, which is one's own Reality. Therefore if, somehow or other, we get the courage to rest the mind perpetually in Him, why worry about other things?

RENUNCIATION

In this chapter the entire effacement of thought is said to be the only true sannyasa (renunciation).

Sannyasa or renunciation is not the discarding of external things but of the ego. To such renouncers (*sannyasins*) there exists no difference between solitude and active life. The Rishi Vasishta says: 'Just as a man, whose mind is preoccupied, is not aware of what is in front of him, so also the Sage, though engaged in work, is not the doer thereof, because his mind is immersed in the Self without the uprising of the ego. Just as a man lying on his bed dreams that he is falling headlong over a precipice, so also the ignorant person whose ego is still present, though engaged in deep meditation in solitude, does not cease to be the doer of all action.'

CONCLUSION

It is within our power to adopt a simple and nutritious diet and, with earnest and incessant endeavour, to eradicate the ego—the cause of all misery—by stopping all mental activity born of the ego.

Can obsessing thoughts arise without the ego, or can there be illusion apart from such thoughts?

2

Who Am I?

'WHO Am I?' was written at the same period as 'Self-Enquiry'. It began as answers to fourteen questions asked by Sivaprakasam Pillai, one of the early disciples. The answers were then formed into this connected exposition. It is the last prose exposition the Maharshi ever wrote. Thereafter he answered enquiries verbally. Records were kept of many of his verbal teachings and some of these have been published by the Asramam in dialogue form, but he himself wrote nothing more except the few verse items that follow in this book. Many of them also were written in answer to some special request.

WHO AM I?

Every living being longs always to be happy, untainted by sorrow; and everyone has the greatest love for himself, which is solely due to the fact that happiness is his real nature. Hence, in order to realize that inherent and untainted happiness, which indeed he daily experiences when the mind is subdued in deep sleep, it is essential that he should know himself. For obtaining such knowledge the enquiry 'Who am I?' in quest of the Self is the best means.

'WHO AM I?' I am not this physical body, nor am I the five organs of sense perception;[1] I am not the five organs of external activity,[2] nor am I the five vital forces,[3] nor am I even the thinking

---

[1] The eye, ear, nose, tongue, and skin, with their respective corresponding functions of sight, hearing, smell, taste, and touch.

[2] The vocal organs that articulate speech and produce sound, hands and feet that govern the movements of the physical body, anus that excretes faecal matter, and the genital organ which yields pleasure.

[3] Which control respiration, digestion and assimilation, circulation of blood, perspiration, and excretion.

mind. Neither am I that unconscious state of nescience which retains merely the subtle *vasanas* (latencies of the mind), while being
free from the functional activity of the sense-organs and of the
mind, and being unaware of the existence of the objects of sense-
perception.

Therefore, summarily rejecting all the above-mentioned physical
adjuncts and their functions, saying 'I am not this; no, nor am I this,
nor this'—that which then remains separate and alone by itself, that
pure Awareness is what I am. This Awareness is by its very nature
Sat-Chit-Ananda (Existence-Consciousness-Bliss).

If the mind, which is the instrument of knowledge and is the
basis of all activity, subsides, the perception of the world as an objective reality ceases. Unless the illusory perception of the serpent
in the rope ceases, the rope on which the illusion is formed is not
perceived as such.[1] Similarly, unless the illusory nature of the perception of the world as an objective reality ceases, the Vision of
the true nature of the Self, on which the illusion is formed, is not
obtained.

The mind is a unique power (*sakti*) in the Atman, whereby
thoughts occur to one. On scrutiny as to what remains after eliminat-
ing all thoughts, it will be found that there is no such thing as mind
apart from thought. So then, thoughts themselves constitute the
mind.

Nor is there any such thing as the physical world apart from and
independent of thought. In deep sleep there are no thoughts: nor is
there the world. In the wakeful and dream state thoughts are present,
and there is also the world. Just as the spider draws out the thread of
the cobweb from within itself and withdraws it again into itself, in
the same way the mind projects the world out of itself and absorbs
it back into itself.

The world is perceived as an apparent objective reality when the
mind is externalized, thereby forsaking its identity with the Self.
When the world is thus perceived, the true nature of the Self is not
revealed: conversely, when the Self is realized, the world ceases to
appear as an objective reality.

By a steady and continuous investigation into the nature of the

---

[1] This analogy is based on a traditional story of a man who sees a rope in the twilight and
mistakes it for a serpent and is therefore afraid without cause.

mind, the mind is transformed into *That* to which the 'I' refers; and that is in fact the Self. Mind has necessarily to depend for its existence on something gross; it never subsists by itself. It is this mind that is otherwise called the subtle body, ego, *jiva* or soul.

That which arises in the physical body as 'I' is the mind. If one enquires whence the 'I'-thought in the body arises in the first instance, it will be found that it is from *hrdayam*[1] or the Heart. That is the source and stay of the mind. Or again, even if one merely continuously repeats to oneself inwardly 'I-I' with the entire mind fixed thereon, that also leads one to the same source.

The first and foremost of all the thoughts that arise in the mind is the primal 'I'-thought. It is only after the rise or origin of the 'I'-thought that innumerable other thoughts arise. In other words, only after the first personal pronoun, 'I', has arisen, do the second and third personal pronouns ('you, he,' etc.) occur to the mind; and they cannot subsist without the former.

Since every other thought can occur only after the rise of the 'I'-thought and since the mind is nothing but a bundle of thoughts, it is only through the enquiry 'Who am I?' that the mind subsides. Moreover, the integral 'I'-thought, implicit in such enquiry, having destroyed all other thoughts, gets itself finally destroyed or consumed, just as the stick used for stirring the burning funeral pyre gets consumed.

Even when extraneous thoughts sprout up during such enquiry, do not seek to complete the rising thought, but instead, deeply enquire within, 'To whom has this thought occurred?' No matter how many thoughts thus occur to you, if you would with acute vigilance enquire immediately as and when each individual thought arises to whom it has occurred, you would find it is to 'me'. If then you enquire 'Who am I?' the mind gets introverted and the rising thought also subsides. In this manner as you persevere more and more in the practice of Self-enquiry, the mind acquires increasing strength and power to abide in its Source.

It is only when the subtle mind is externalized through the activity of the intellect and the sense-organs that gross name and form constituting the world appear. When, on the other hand, the

---

[1] The word '*hrdayam*' consists of two syllables, '*hrt*' and '*ayam*', which signify 'I am the Heart'.

mind stays firmly in the Heart, they recede and disappear. Restraint of the out-going mind and its absorption in the Heart is known as introversion (*antarmukha-drishti*). The release of the mind and its emergence from the Heart is known as *bahirmukha-drishti* (objectiveness).

If in this manner the mind becomes absorbed in the Heart, the ego or 'I', which is the centre of the multitude of thoughts, finally vanishes and pure Consciousness or Self, which subsists during all the states of the mind, alone remains resplendent. It is this state, where there is not the slightest trace of the 'I'-thought, that is the true Being of oneself. And that is called Quiescence or *Mouna* (Silence).

This state of mere inherence in pure Being is known as the Vision of Wisdom. Such inherence means and implies the entire subsidence of the mind in the Self. Nothing other than this and no psychic powers of the mind, such as thought-reading, telepathy and clairvoyance, can be Wisdom.

Atman alone exists and is real. The threefold reality of world, individual soul, and God is, like the illusory appearance of silver in the mother of pearl, an imaginary creation in the Atman. They appear and disappear simultaneously. The Self alone is the world, the 'I' and God. All that exists is but the manifestation of the Supreme.

For the subsidence of mind there is no other means more effective and adequate than Self-enquiry. Even though by other means the mind subsides, that is only apparently so; it will rise again.

For instance, the mind subsides by the practice of *pranayama* (restraint and control of breath and vital forces); yet such subsidence lasts only as long as the control of breath and vital forces continues; and when they are released, the mind also gets released and immediately, becoming externalized, it continues to wander through the force of its subtle tendencies.

The source of the mind is the same as that of breath and vital forces. It is really the multitude of thoughts that constitutes the mind; and the 'I'-thought is the primal thought of the mind, and is itself the ego. But breath too has its origin at the same place whence the ego rises. Therefore, when the mind subsides, breath and vital forces also subside; and conversely, when the latter subside, the former also subsides.

Breath and vital forces are also described as the gross manifestation of the mind. Till the hour of death the mind sustains and supports these forces in the physical body; and when life becomes extinct the mind envelops them and carries them away. During sleep, however, the vital forces continue to function, although the mind is not manifest. This is according to the divine law and is intended to protect the body and to remove any possible doubt as to whether it is dead or alive while one is asleep. Without such arrangement by nature, sleeping bodies would often be cremated alive. The vitality apparent in breathing is left behind by the mind as a 'watchman'. But in the wakeful state and in *samadhi*, when the mind subsides, breath also subsides. For this reason (because the mind has the sustaining and controlling power over breath and vital forces and is therefore ulterior to both of them), the practice of breath-control is merely helpful in subduing the mind but cannot bring about its final extinction.

Like breath-control, meditation on form, incantations, invocations and regulation of diet are only aids to control of the mind. Through the practice of meditation or invocation the mind becomes one-pointed. Just as the elephant's trunk, which is otherwise restless, will become steady if it is made to hold an iron chain, so that the elephant goes its way without reaching out for any other object, so also the ever-restless mind, which is trained and accustomed to a name or form through meditation or invocation, will steadily hold on to that alone.

When the mind is split up and dissipated into countless varying thoughts, each individual thought becomes extremely weak and inefficient. When, on the contrary, such thoughts subside more and more till they finally get destroyed, the mind becomes one-pointed and, thereby acquiring strength and power of endurance, easily reaches perfection in the method of enquiry in quest of the Self.

Regulation of diet, restricting it to *satvic* food,[1] taken in moderate quantity, is of all the rules of conduct the best; and it is most conducive to the development of the *satvic* qualities[2] of the mind. These,

---

[1] i.e. simple and nutritious food which sustains but does not stimulate the physical body.

[2] Purity of heart, self-restraint, evenness of temper, tenderness towards all beings, fortitude and freedom from desire, hatred and arrogance are the outstanding virtues of the *satvic* mind.

in their turn, assist one in the practice of *Atma vichara* or enquiry in quest of the Self.

Countless *vishaya-vasanas* (subtle tendencies of the mind in relation to objects of sense-gratification), coming one after the other in quick succession like the waves of the ocean, agitate the mind. Nevertheless, they too subside and finally get destroyed with progressive practice of *Atma dhyana* or meditation on the Self. Without giving room even to the thought which occurs in the form of doubt, whether it is possible to stay merely as the very Self, whether all the *vasanas* can be destroyed, one should firmly and unceasingly carry on meditation on the Self.

However sinful a person may be, if he would stop wailing inconsolably: 'Alas! I am a sinner, how shall I attain Liberation?' and, casting away even the thought that he is a sinner, if he would zealously carry on meditation on the Self, he would most assuredly get reformed.

So long as subtle tendencies continue to inhere in the mind, it is necessary to carry on the enquiry: 'Who am I?' As and when thoughts occur, they should, one and all, be annihilated then and there, at the very place of their origin, by the method of enquiry in quest of the Self.

Not to desire anything extraneous to oneself constitutes *vairagya* (dispassion) or *nirasa* (desirelessness). Not to give up one's hold on the Self constitutes *jnana* (knowledge). But really *vairagya* and *jnana* are one and the same. Just as the pearl-diver, tying stones to his waist, dives down into the depths, and gets the pearl from the seabed, so every aspirant pledged to *vairagya* can dive deep into himself and realize the precious Atman. If the earnest seeker would only cultivate the constant and deep contemplative 'remembrance' (*smrti*) of the true nature of the Self till he has realized it, that alone would suffice. Distracting thoughts are like the enemy in the fortress. As long as they are in possession of it, they will certainly sally forth. But if, as and when they come out, you put them to the sword the fortress will finally be captured.

God and the Guru are not really different: they are identical. He that has earned the Grace of the Guru shall undoubtedly be saved and never forsaken, just as the prey that has fallen into the tiger's jaws will never be allowed to escape. But the disciple, for his part, should unswervingly follow the path shown by the Master.

Firm and disciplined inherence in the Atman without giving the least scope for the rise of any thought other than the deep contemplative thought of the Self, constitutes self-surrender to the Supreme Lord. Let any amount of burden be laid on Him, He will bear it all. It is, in fact, the indefinable power of the Lord that ordains, sustains and controls everything that happens. Why then should we worry, tormented by vexatious thoughts, saying: 'Shall we act this way? No, that way,' instead of meekly but happily submitting to that Power? Knowing that the train carries all the weight, why indeed should we, the passengers travelling in it, carry our small individual articles of luggage on our laps to our great discomfort, instead of putting them aside and sitting at perfect ease?

That which is Bliss is also the Self. Bliss and the Self are not distinct and separate but are one and the same. And *That* alone is real. In no single one of the countless objects of the mundane world is there anything that can be called happiness. It is through sheer ignorance and unwisdom that we fancy that happiness is obtained from them. On the contrary, when the mind is externalized, it suffers pain and anguish. The truth is that every time our desires get fulfilled, the mind, turning to its source, experiences only that happiness which is natural to the Self. Similarly, in deep sleep, in spiritual trance (*samadhi*), when fainting, when a desired object is obtained, or when evil befalls an object considered undesirable, the mind turns inwards and enjoys that Bliss of Atman. Thus wandering astray, forsaking the Self, and returning to it again and again is the interminable and wearisome lot of the mind.

It is pleasant under the shade of a tree and scorching in the heat of the sun outside. A person toiling in the sun seeks the cool shade of the tree and is happy under it. After staying there for a while, he moves out again but, unable to bear the merciless heat of the sun, he again seeks the shade. In this way he keeps on moving from shade to sun and sun to shade.

It is an unwise person who acts thus, whereas the wise man never leaves the shade: in the same way the mind of the Enlightened Sage (*Jnani*) never exists apart from Brahman, the Absolute. The mind of the ignorant, on the other hand, entering into the phenomenal world, suffers pain and anguish; and then, turning for a short while towards Brahman, it experiences happiness. Such is the mind of the ignorant.

This phenomenal world, however, is nothing but thought. When the world recedes from one's view—that is when one is free from thought—the mind enjoys the Bliss of the Self. Conversely, when the world appears—that is when thought occurs—the mind experiences pain and anguish.

Not from any desire, resolve, or effort on the part of the rising sun, but merely due to the presence of his rays, the lens emits heat, the lotus blossoms, water evaporates, and people attend to their various duties in life. In the promixity of the magnet the needle moves. Similarly the soul or *jiva*, subjected to the threefold activity of creation, preservation, and destruction which take place merely due to the unique Presence of the Supreme Lord, performs acts in accordance with its karma,[1] and subsides to rest after such activity. But the Lord Himself has no resolve; no act or event touches even the fringe of His Being. This state of immaculate aloofness can be likened to that of the sun, which is untouched by the activities of life, or to that of the all-pervasive ether, which is not affected by the interaction of the complex qualities of the other four elements.

All scriptures without any exception proclaim that for attaining Salvation the mind should be subdued; and once one knows that control of the mind is their final aim, it is futile to make an interminable study of them. What is required for such control is actual enquiry into oneself by self-interrogation: 'Who am I?' How can this enquiry in quest of the Self be made merely by means of a study of the scriptures?

One should realize the Self by the Eye of Wisdom. Does Rama need a mirror to recognize himself as Rama? That to which the 'I' refers is within the five sheaths,[2] whereas the scriptures are outside them. Therefore, it is futile to seek by means of the study of scriptures the Self that has to be realized by summarily rejecting even the five sheaths.

To enquire 'Who am I that is in bondage?' and to know one's

---

[1] i.e. the fruits of past actions which are being worked out in the present life.
[2] These are the physical, vital, and mental sheaths, and the sheaths of Knowledge-Experience and of Bliss.

real nature is alone Liberation. To keep the mind constantly turned within and to abide thus in the Self is alone *Atma-vichara* (Self-enquiry), whereas *dhyana* (meditation) consists in fervent contemplation of the Self as *Sat-Chit-Ananda* (Being-Consciousness-Bliss). Indeed, at some time, one will have to forget everything that has been learnt.

Just as it is futile to examine the rubbish that has to be swept up only to be thrown away, so it is futile for him who seeks to know the Self to set to work enumerating the *tattvas*[1] that envelop the Self and examining them instead of casting them away. He should consider the phenomenal world with reference to himself as merely a dream.

Except that the wakeful state is long and the dream state is short, there is no difference beween the two. All the activities of the dream state appear, for the time being, just as real as the activities of the wakeful state seem to be while awake. Only, during the dream state, the mind assumes another form or a different bodily sheath. For thoughts on the one hand and name and form on the other occur simultaneously during both the wakeful and dream states.

There are not two minds, one good and the other evil. It is only the *vasanas* or tendencies of the mind that are of two kinds, good and favourable, evil and unfavourable. When the mind is associated with the former it is called good; and when associated with the latter it is called evil. However evil-minded other people may appear to you, it is not proper to hate or despise them. Likes and dislikes, love and hatred are equally to be eschewed. It is also not proper to let the mind often rest on objects or affairs of mundane life. As far as possible one should not interfere in the affairs of others. Everything offered to others is really an offering to oneself; and if only this truth were realized, who is there that would refuse anything to others?

If the ego rises, all else will also rise; if it subsides, all else will also subside. The deeper the humility with which we conduct ourselves, the better it is for us. If only the mind is kept under control, what matters it where one may happen to be?

---

[1] *Tattvas* are the elements into which phenomenal existence—from the subtle mind to gross matter—is classified.

3

Five Hymns to Sri Arunachala

THE Five Hymns to Arunachala are the earliest poems of the
Maharshi except for a few short verses. They were written
about 1914, that is when he was about thirty-five years of age
(he was born in December 1879). He was still living in a cave on the
hill. Some of his followers who were sadhus used to go into the town
of Tiruvannamalai daily to beg for food and one day they asked him
to make a song for them to sing as they went. At first he refused,
saying that there were plenty of songs already made by the ancient
Saivite Saints. They continued to press him, however, and one day
he walked round the hill, composing the first hymn, the Marital
Garland of Letters, as he went. It tells in glowing symbolism of the
love and union between the human soul and God and is among the
most profound and moving poems in any language. Although he
who wrote it was established in the Bliss of indissoluble Union, it
was written for the sake of devotees and expresses the attitude of the
soul that still aspires.

The second, third, and fourth poems were written at about the
same time, and they also adopt the same attitude. Whereas the later
poems of the Maharshi are more doctrinal, these hymns are more
emotional, expressing more the attitude of devotion and aspira-
tion.

The *Eleven Verses* and the *Eight Verses* are among the very few
poems of the Maharshi that were written quite spontaneously without any request. As he himself said when speaking of them:

'The only poems that came to me spontaneously and com-
pelled me, as it were, to write them without anyone urging me
to do so are the *Eleven Stanzas to Sri Arunachala* and the *Eight
Stanzas to Sri Arunachala*. The opening words of the *Eleven*

Stanzas came to me one morning and even though I tried to suppress them, saying 'What have I to do with these words?' they would not be suppressed till I composed a song bringing them in; and all the words flowed easily, without any effort. In the same way the second stanza was made the next day and the succeeding ones the following days, one each day. Only the tenth and eleventh were composed the same day.'[1]

He went on to describe in his characteristically vivid way how he composed the *Eight Stanzas*:

'The next day I started out to go round the hill. Palaniswami was walking behind me and after we had gone some way Aiyasami seems to have called him back and given him a pencil and paper, saying, "For some days now Swami has been composing poems every day. He may do so today as well, so you had better take this paper and pencil with you."

I learnt about this only when I noticed that Palaniswami was not with me for a while but caught me up later. That day, before I got back to Virupaksha, I wrote six of the eight stanzas. Either that evening or the next day Narayana Reddi came. He was at that time living in Vellore as an agent of Singer & Co., and he used to come from time to time. Aiyasami and Palani told him about the poems and he said, "Give them to me at once and I will go and get them printed." He had already published some books. When he insisted on taking the poems I told him he could do so and could publish the first eleven as one form of poem and the rest, which were in a different metre, as another. To make up the required quota I at once composed two more stanzas and he took all the nineteen stanzas with him to get them published.'

The fifth hymn is of a different nature to the first four. The great Sanskrit poet and devotee Ganapati Sastri, who was a follower of Bhagavan, begged him to write a poem in Sanskrit. Bhagavan replied, laughing, that he scarcely knew any Sanskrit and no Sanskrit

[1] *Ramana Maharshi and the Path of Self-Knowledge*, pp. 171-2 by Arthur Osborne, (Samuel Weiser, 1995).

metres. Sastri, however, explained a metre to him and repeated his request. When he returned the same evening this hymn had been written in perfect, flawless Sanskrit. It is a cryptic account of the different paths to Realization and therefore a commentary has been included with the translation.

It is to be understood that in all these hymns the word '*Aruna-chala*' means God and nothing less. It also, however, means the physical hill of Arunachala in South India where God is peculiarly manifested for the Maharshi and his disciples. From ancient times various spiritual centres in India have represented various spiritual paths and modes of doctrine, and Arunachala among them the doctrine of Advaita and the path of Self-enquiry. Although the ultimate doctrine and the supreme and most direct path, this, throughout the ages, has not been the most popular, because for most people it seemed too austere and difficult. The Maharshi attained Realization through a spontaneous act of Self-enquiry, with no human Guru. There is no place to do more than touch upon the mystery of this here. It is sufficient to note that the Maharshi agreed with all other Masters that a Guru is necessary, adding however that the Guru need not necessarily take human form. When he left home as a youth who was already a Sage, Arunachala drew him like a powerful magnet. He went straight there and stayed there for the rest of his life. It was Arunachala that he regarded as his Guru, and these hymns are written to Arunachala, to the Guru, to God Manifested, to the Absolute.

Through the potent Grace of Bhagavan Ramana Maharshi, the path of Self-enquiry was brought within the competence of men and women of this age, was indeed fashioned into a new path that can be followed anonymously in the conditions of the modern world, with no forms or ritual, nothing to distinguish a person outwardly from the world wherein he moves. This creation of a new path to suit the needs of the age has made Arunachala the spiritual centre of the world. More than ever, now that he has shed his physical body and is one with Arunachala, the Grace and guidance that emanates from him to those who turn to him and seek his aid is centred at Arunachala. It is the holy place and many are drawn there, both those who were disciples of the Maharshi in his lifetime and those who have come later.

It remains to be said that the literary Tamil in which the hymns were written can be used in an extremely cryptic manner and the first hymn especially abounds in passages which can be understood in more than one manner. In such cases the alternative readings are given.

* * * * *

SRI ARUNACHALA MAHATMYA[1]

THE GLORY OF SRI ARUNACHALA

Nandi[2] said:

'That is the holy place! Of all Arunachala is the most sacred! It is the heart of the world! Know it to be the secret and sacred Heart-centre of Siva! In that place He always abides as the glorious Aruna Hill!'

Siva said:

'Though in fact fiery, my lack-lustre appearance as a hill on this spot is an effect of grace and loving solicitude for the maintenance of the world. Here I always abide as the Great One (*Siddha*). Remember that in the interior of My Heart is transcendental glory with all the enjoyments of the world also.

'This glorious Arunachala is that of which the mere sight suffices to remove all demerits which divide up Being into egos and finite worlds.

'What cannot be acquired without endless pains—the true import of the Vedanta—is easily attained by all who can either directly sight this Hill or even mentally think of it from afar.

'I ordain that residence within a radius of three *Yojanas*[3] of this Hill shall by itself suffice to burn off all defects and effect union with the Supreme (even in the absence of initiation).'

---

[1] Extracts from *The Skanda Purana.*
[2] Nandi is the foremost devotee of Siva always remaining in front of him.
[3] *Yojana*—10 miles.

THE MARITAL GARLAND OF LETTERS

INVOCATION

Gracious Ganapati! with Thy (loving) hand bless me, that I may make this a marital garland of letters worthy of Sri Arunachala, the Bridegroom!

REFRAIN

Arunachala Shiva! Arunachala Shiva!
Arunachala Shiva! Arunachala!
Arunachala Shiva! Arunachala Shiva!
Arunachala Shiva! Arunachala!

1(a) Arunachala! Thou dost root out the ego of those who meditate on Thee in the heart, Oh Arunachala!

(b) Arunachala! Thou dost root out the ego of those who dwell on their (spiritual) identity with Thee, Oh Arunachala!

2. May Thou and I be one and inseparable like *Alagu* and *Sundara*,[1] Oh Arunachala!

3. Entering (my) home and luring me (to Thine), why didst Thou keep me prisoner in Thy heart's cavern, Oh Arunachala?

4. Was it for Thy pleasure or for my sake Thou didst win me? If now Thou turn me away, the world will blame Thee, Oh Arunachala!

5. Escape this blame! Why didst Thou then recall Thyself to me? How can I leave Thee now, Oh Arunachala?

6(a) Kinder far art Thou than one's own mother. Is this then Thy all-kindness, Oh Arunachala?

(b) Kinder indeed art Thou than one's own mother, such is Thy Love, Oh Arunachala!

7(a) Sit firmly in my mind lest it elude Thee, Oh Arunachala!

---

[1] The Tamil word *alagu* and Sanskrit word *sundara* have the same meaning: 'beauty'. Alagu and Sundara were also the names of Sri Ramana's mother and father.

(b) Change not Thy nature and flee, but hold fast in my mind, Oh Arunachala!

(c) Be watchful in my mind, lest it change even Thee (into me) and rush away, Oh Arunachala!

8(a) Display Thy beauty, for the fickle mind to see Thee for ever and to rest (in peace), Oh Arunachala!

(b) The strumpet mind will cease to walk the streets if only she find Thee. Disclose Thy Beauty then and hold her bound, Oh Arunachala!

(c) The mind by her unsteadiness prevents my seeking Thee and finding peace; (hold her and) grant me the vision of Thy Beauty, Oh Arunachala!

9. After abducting me if now Thou dost not embrace me, where is Thy chivalry, Oh Arunachala?

10. Does it become Thee thus to sleep when I am outraged by others, Oh Arunachala?

11. Even when the thieves of the five senses break in upon me, art Thou not still in my heart, Oh Arunachala!

12. One art Thou without a second; who then could dare elude Thee and come in? This is only Thy jugglery, Oh Arunachala!

13. Significance of OM unrivalled—unsurpassed! Who can comprehend Thee, Oh Arunachala?

14. As (Universal) Mother, it is Thy duty to dispense Thy Grace and save me, Oh Arunachala!

15(a) Who can ever find Thee? The Eye of the eye art Thou, and without eyes Thou seest, Oh Arunachala!

(b) Being the sight of the eye, even without eyes find me out Thyself. Who (but Thyself) can find out Thee, Oh Arunachala?

16. As a lode-stone attracts iron, magnetizing it and holding it fast, so do Thou to me, Oh Arunachala!

17. (Unmoving) Hill, melting into a Sea of Grace, have mercy (on me) I pray, Oh Arunachala!

18. Fiery Gem, shining in all directions, do Thou burn up my dross, Oh Arunachala!

19. Shine as my Guru, making me free from faults and worthy of Thy Grace, Oh Arunachala!

20. Save me from the cruel snares of fascinating women and honour me with union with Thyself, Oh Arunachala!

21. Though I beg, Thou art callous and dost not condescend. I pray Thee! say to me 'Fear not!' Oh Arunachala!

22. Unasked Thou givest; this is Thy imperishable fame. Do not belie Thy name, Oh Arunachala!

23. Sweet fruit within my hands, let me be mad with ecstasy, drunk with the Bliss of Thy Essence, Oh Arunachala!

24. Blazoned as the Devourer of Thy votaries, how can I survive who have embraced Thee, Oh Arunachala?

25(a) Thou, unruffled by anger! What crime has marked me off (for Thy wrath), Oh Arunachala?

(b) Thou, unruffled by anger! What (austerities left) incomplete (in previous births) have won me Thy special favour, Oh Arunachala?

26. Glorious Mountain of Love, celebrated by Gautama,[1] rule me with Thy gracious glance, Oh Arunachala!

27. Dazzling Sun that swallowest up all the universe in Thy rays, in Thy Light open the lotus of my heart I pray, Oh Arunachala!

28(a) Let me, Thy prey, surrender unto Thee and be consumed, and so have Peace, Oh Arunachala!

(b) I came to feed on Thee, but Thou hast fed on me; now there is Peace, Oh Arunachala!

29. O Moon of Grace, with Thy (cool) rays as hands, open (within me) the ambrosial orifice and let my heart rejoice, Arunachala!

30. Tear off these robes, expose me naked, then robe me with Thy Love, Oh Arunachala!

31. There (in the heart) rest quiet! Let the sea of joy surge, speech and feeling cease, Oh Arunachala!

32. Do not continue to deceive and prove me; disclose instead Thy Transcendental Self, Oh Arunachala!

33. Vouchsafe the knowledge of Eternal Life that I may learn the glorious Primal Wisdom, and shun the delusion of this world, Oh Arunachala!

34. Unless Thou embrace me, I shall melt away in tears of anguish, Oh Arunachala!

[1] The Gautama here referred to is not the Buddha but a Hindu Sage of that name who dwelt at Arunachala.

35. If spurned by Thee, alas! what rests for me but the torment of my *prarabdha*?[1] What hope is left for me, Arunachala?

36. In silence Thou saidst, 'Stay silent!' and Thyself stood silent, Oh Arunachala![2]

37. Happiness lies in peaceful repose enjoyed when resting in the Self. Beyond speech indeed is This my State, Oh Arunachala!

38(a) Thou didst display Thy prowess once, and, the perils ended, return to Thy repose, Oh Arunachala!

(b) Sun! Thou didst sally forth and (the siege of) illusion was ended. Then didst Thou shine motionless (alone), Oh Arunachala!

39(a) (A dog can scent out its master); am I then worse than a dog? Steadfastly will I seek Thee and regain Thee, Oh Arunachala!

(b) Worse than a dog (for want of scent), how can I track Thee (to Thy home), Oh Arunachala?

40. Grant me wisdom, I beseech Thee, so that I may not pine for love of Thee in ignorance, Oh Arunachala!

41(a) Not finding the flower open, Thou didst stay, no better than a bee (trapped in the bud of my mind), Oh Arunachala!

(b) (In sunlight the lotus blossoms), how then couldst Thou, the Sun of suns, hover before me like a flower bee, saying 'Thou art not yet in blossom', Oh Arunachala?

42(a) 'Thou hast realized the Self even without knowing that it was the Truth. It is the Truth Itself!' Speak (thus if it be so), Oh Arunachala!

(b) Thou art the subject of most diverse views yet art Thou not this only, Oh Arunachala?

(c) Not known to the *tattvas*, though Thou art their being! What does this mean, Oh Arunachala?

43(a) That each one is Reality Itself, Thou wilt of Thy Nature show, Oh Arunachala!

(b) Reveal Thyself! Thou only art Reality, Oh Arunachala!

(c) 'Reality is nothing but the Self'; is this not all Thy message, Oh Arunachala?

44. 'Look within, ever seeking the Self with the inner eye, then

---

[1] *Prarabdha* is the part of destiny due to past actions (*karmas*) which bears fruit in the present birth.

[2] Silence is the highest and most perfect form of instruction which the *Guru* can give, for by its nature it is closest to the essential object of such instruction, which is the realization by the disciple of the incommunicable and inexpressible Absolute.

will (It) be found.' Thus didst Thou direct me, beloved Arunachala!

45(a) Seeking Thee within but weakly, I came back (unrewarded). Aid me, Oh Arunachala!

(b) Weak though my effort was, by Thy Grace I gained the Self, Oh Arunachala!

(c) Seeking Thee in the Infinite Self, I regained my own (Self), Oh Arunachala!

46(a) What value has this birth without Knowledge born of realization? It is not even worth speaking about, Oh Arunachala!

47(a) Let me dive into the true Self, wherein merge only the pure in mind and speech, Oh Arunachala!

(b) I, by Thy Grace, am sunk in Thy Self, wherein merge only those divested of their minds and thus made pure, Oh Arunachala!

48. When I took shelter under Thee as my One God, Thou didst destroy me altogether, Oh Arunachala!

49. Treasure of benign and holy Grace, found without seeking, steady my wandering mind, Oh Arunachala!

50. On seeking Thy Real Self with courage, my raft capsized and the waters came over me. Have mercy on me Arunachala!

51(a) Unless Thou extend Thy hand of Grace in mercy and embrace me, I am lost, Oh Arunachala!

(b) Enfold me body to body, limb to limb, or I am lost, Oh Arunachala!

52. O Undefiled, abide Thou in my heart so that there may be everlasting joy, Arunachala!

53(a) Mock me not, who seek Thy protection! Adorn me with Thy Grace and then regard me, Oh Arunachala!

(b) Smile with Grace and not with scorn on me, who come to Thee (for refuge), Oh Arunachala!

54(a) When I approached, Thou didst not bend; Thou stoodst unmoved, at one with me, Oh Arunachala!

(b) Does it not shame Thee to stand there like a post, (leaving me) to find Thee by myself, Oh Arunachala?

55. Rain Thy Mercy on me ere Thy Knowledge burn me to ashes, Oh Arunachala!

56. Unite with me to destroy (our separate identities as) Thou and me, and bless me with the state of ever-vibrant joy, Oh Arunachala!

57(a) When shall I (become) like the ether and reach Thee, subtle of being, that the tempest of thoughts may end, Oh Arunachala?

(b) When will waves of thought cease to rise? When shall I reach Thee, subtler than the subtle ether, Oh Arunachala!

58(a) I am a simpleton devoid of learning. Do Thou dispel illusion, Oh Arunachala!

(b) Destroy Thou my wrong knowledge, I beseech Thee, for I lack the knowledge which the Scriptures lead to, Oh Arunachala!

59. When I melted away and entered Thee, my Refuge, (I found) Thee standing naked (like the famous *Digambara*),[1] Oh Arunachala!

60. In my unloving self Thou didst create a passion for Thee, therefore forsake me not, Oh Arunachala!

61(a) Fruit shrivelled and spoilt is worthless; take and enjoy it ripe, Oh Arunachala!

(b) I am not (like) a fruit which is overripe and spoilt; draw me, then, into the inmost recess (of the heart) and fix me in Eternity, Oh Arunachala!

62(a) Hast Thou not bartered cunningly Thyself for me (for my individuality is lost)? Oh, Thou art death to me, Arunachala!

(b) Hast thou not bartered happily Thyself for me (giving all and taking nothing)? Art Thou not blind, Oh Arunachala?

63. Regard me! Take thought of me! Touch me![2] Mature me! Make me one with Thee, Oh Arunachala!

64. Grant me Thy Grace ere the poison of delusion grips me and, rising to my head, kills me, Oh Arunachala!

65. Thyself regard me and dispel illusion! Unless Thou do so who can intercede with Grace Itself made manifest, Oh Arunachala?

66. With madness for Thee hast Thou freed me of madness (for the world); grant me now the cure of all madness, Oh Arunachala!

67. Fearless I seek Thee, Fearlessness Itself! How canst Thou fear to take me, Oh Arunachala?

68. Where is (my) ignorance or (Thy) Wisdom, if I am blessed with union to Thee, Oh Arunachala?

69(a) My mind has blossomed, (then) scent it with Thy fragrance and perfect it. Oh Arunachala!

---

[1] *Digambara*, from *dik*—the directions of space, and *ambara*—cloth, i.e. one who is clothed in the directions of space, in other words, who goes naked.

[2] 'Regard me! Take thought of me! Touch me!' refer respectively to the three modes of initiation, by look, by thought, and by touch.

(b) Espouse me, I beseech Thee, and let this mind, now wedded to the world, be wedded to Perfection, Oh Arunachala!

70. Mere thought of Thee has drawn me to Thee, and who can gauge Thy Glory (in Itself), Oh Arunachala?

71. Thou hast possessed me, unexorcizable Spirit! and made me mad (for Thee), that I may cease to be a ghost (wandering the world), Oh Arunachala!

72. Be Thou my stay and my support lest I droop helpless like a tender creeper, Oh Arunachala!

73. Thou didst benumb (my faculties) with stupefying powder,[1] then rob me of my understanding and reveal the Knowledge of Thy self, Oh Arunachala!

74. Show me the warfare of Thy Grace, in the Open Field where there is no coming and going. Oh Arunachala!

75. Unattached to the physical frame composed of the (five) elements, let me for ever repose happy in the sight of Thy Splendour, Oh Arunachala!

76. Thou hast administered the medicine of confusion to me, so must I be confounded! Shine Thou as Grace, the cure of all confusion, Oh Arunachala!

77. Shine Thou selfless, sapping the pride of those who boast of their free will, Oh Arunachala!

78. I am a fool who prays only when overwhelmed (by misery), yet disappoint me not, Oh Arunachala!

79. Guard me lest I flounder storm-tossed like a ship without helmsman, Oh Arunachala!

80. Thou hast cut the knot which hid the vision of Thy Head and Foot (the limitless Self). Motherlike, shouldst Thou not complete Thy task, Oh Arunachala?[2]

81. Be not (like) a mirror held up to a noseless man, but raise me (from my lowness) and embrace me, Oh Arunachala!

82. Let us embrace upon the bed of tender flowers, which is the mind, within the room of the body (or the Ultimate Truth), Oh Arunachala!

---

[1] This verse alludes to the wandering ascetics who spirit away children for disciples, stupefying them with a pinch of powder, such as sacred ashes.

[2] The cutting of the knot which binds man to illusion implies the attainment of *nirvikalpa samadhi*; completion of the task refers to the state of *sahaja samadhi*.

83. How is it that Thou hast become famous from Thy constant union with the poor and humble, Oh Arunachala?

84. Thou hast removed the blindness of ignorance with the unguent of Thy Grace, and made me truly Thine, Oh Arunachala!

85. Thou didst shave clean my head (and I was lost to the world);[1] then Thou didst (show Thyself) dancing in Transcendent Space, Oh Arunachala!

86(a) Though Thou hast loosed me from the mists of error and made me mad for Thee, why hast Thou not yet freed me from illusion, Oh Arunachala?

(b) Though Thou hast detached me from the world and made me cleave to Thee, Thy passion for me has not cooled, Oh Arunachala!

87. Is it true Silence to rest like a stone, inert and unexpansive, Oh Arunachala?

88. Who was it that threw mud to me for food[2] and robbed me of my livelihood, Oh Arunachala?

89. Unknown to all, stupefying me, Who was it that ravished my soul, Oh Arunachala?

90. I spoke thus to Thee, because Thou art my Lord; be not offended but come and give me happiness, Oh Arunachala!

91. Let us enjoy one another in the House of Open Space, where there is neither night nor day, Oh Arunachala![3]

92. Thou didst take aim (at me) with darts of Love and then devoured me alive, Oh Arunachala!

93. Thou art the Primal Being, whereas I count not in this nor in the other world. What didst Thou gain then by my worthless self, Oh Arunachala?

94. Didst Thou not call me in? I have come in. Now measure out for me, (my maintenance is now Thy burden). Hard is Thy lot, Oh Arunachala!

95. The moment Thou didst welcome me, didst enter into me and grant me Thy divine life, I lost my individuality, Oh Arunachala!

---

[1] The parenthesis is not a mere addition to explain the implication of shaving the head, for by an alternative reading, involving the change of a single letter, these words become explicit in the text.

[2] Literally, 'Threw mud in my mouth', an expression meaning 'caused my ruin'. The deeper meaning of this verse is: 'Who was it that individualized me and robbed me of my Perfect Being?'

[3] The allusion is to the 'cavity of the Heart' which is beyond time and space.

96. Bless me that I may die without losing hold of Thee, or miserable is (my fate), Oh Arunachala!

97. From my home Thou didst entice me, then stealing into my heart didst draw me gently into Thine, (such is) Thy Grace, Oh Arunachala!

98. I have betrayed Thy (secret) workings. Be not offended! Show me Thy Grace now openly and save me, Oh Arunachala!

99. Grant me the essence of the Vedas, which shine in the Vedanta, One without a second, Oh Arunachala!

100(a) Even my slanders, treat as praise and guard me for ever as Thine own, I pray, Oh Arunachala!

   (b) Let even slander be as praise to me, and guard me for ever as Thine own, I pray, Oh Arunachala!

   (c) Place (Thy hand) upon my head! make me partaker of Thy Grace! do not abandon me, I pray, Oh Arunachala!

101. As snow in water, let me melt as Love in Thee, Who art Love itself, Oh Arunachala!

102. I had but thought of Thee as Aruna, and lo! I was caught in the trap of Thy Grace! Can the net of Thy Grace ever fail, Oh Arunachala?

103. Watching like a spider to trap (me in the web of Thy) Grace, Thou didst entwine me and when imprisoned feed upon me, Oh Arunachala!

104. Let me be the votary of the votaries of those who hear Thy name with love, Oh Arunachala!

105. Shine Thou for ever as the loving Saviour of helpless suppliants like myself, Oh Arunachala!

106. Familiar to Thine ears are the sweet songs of votaries who melt to the very bones with love for Thee, yet let my poor strains also be acceptable, Oh Arunachala!

107. Hill of Patience, bear with my foolish words, (regarding them) as hymns of joy or as Thou please, Oh Arunachala!

108. Oh Arunachala! my Loving Lord! Throw Thy garland (about my shoulders), wearing Thyself this one (strung) by me, Arunachala!

Blessed be Arunachala! blessed be His devotees!
Blessed be this Marital Garland of Letters!

THE NECKLET OF NINE GEMS

1. In the court (of Chidambaram), Siva, though motionless by nature, dances (in rapture) before His Shakti who stands still. Know that in Arunachala He stands in His solemnity and she withdraws there into His Unmoving Self.

2. 'A', 'Ru', and 'Na' signify *Sat*, *Chit*, and *Ananda* (Being, Consciousness, and Bliss), or again the Supreme Self, the individual Self, and their union as the One Absolute, expressed in the *mahavakya*[1] 'That thou art'; 'Achala' signifies Perfection. So worship Arunachala of shining golden lustre; for mere remembrance of Him ensures Deliverance.

3. Those who take refuge at the Lotus Feet of the Supreme Lord of Mercy presiding over Arunachala—their minds freed of attachment to riches, lands and relatives, and to caste and the like,[2] and ever made purer by seeking Thy benign Grace—these rid themselves (of the misery) of darkness, and in the steady light of Thy ever-protecting Grace, which shines like the golden rays of the rising sun, they abide happy, sunk in the Ocean of Bliss.

4. Annamalai![3] think not to let me pine away wistfully as one unmindful of Thee (for Thou art ever in my mind),[4] nor is it (right) that I should be reduced to dust mistaking the vile body for the Self. Turn Thy gracious and refreshing glance upon me, Eye of my eyes! Do not fail me, Lord, Who art Consciousness Itself, neither male nor female. Abide Thou in my Heart!

5. Lord! Who art Consciousness Itself, reigning over the sublime Shonagiri,[5] forgive all the grievous wrongs of this poor self, and by Thy Gracious Glance, benignant as a rain cloud, save me from being lost once more in the dreary waste, or else I cannot ford

---

[1] A *vakya* is a Vedic utterance, four great utterances (*mahavakyas*) are especially distinguished, of which this (TATTVAMASI) is one.
[2] 'The like' are the four stages of life (*ashramas*).
[3] Arunachala.
[4] The parenthesis incorporates an alternative sense.
[5] Arunachala.

the grim (stream of universal) manifestation. (Thou art the Universal Mother);[1] what can match a mother's care for her child?

6. 'Killer of Kama',[2] Thou art always called by Thy votaries. Lord Arunachala! a doubt arises if the title fits Thee. If it is fitting, how then can Kama, the mighty, the invisible, continue, brave and valiant though he be, to creep into a mind sheltering under Thy Feet, Who art his Killer?

7. Oh Arunachala! as soon as Thou didst claim me, my body and soul were Thine. What else can I desire? Thou art both merit and demerit, Oh my Life! I cannot think of these apart from Thee. Do as Thou wilt then, my Beloved, but grant me only ever increasing love for Thy Feet!

8. To rescue me—born of virtuous Sundara and Sundari in the holy place Tiruchuli, seat of Bhuminatheshwara—from the pain of miserable mundane life, He raised me to His state, that His Heart might so rejoice, the immanence of Siva so shine forth, and the Self flourish. Such is Arunachala, famous throughout the universe!

9. Bearing and tending me in the world in the shape of my father and mother, Thou didst abide in my mind, and before I fell into the deep sea called *Jaganmaya*[3] and was drowned, Thou didst draw me to thee, Arunachala, Consciousness Itself, such is the wonder of Thy Grace!

ELEVEN VERSES ON SRI ARUNACHALA

1. Now that by Thy Grace Thou hast claimed me, what will become of me unless Thou manifest Thyself to me, and I, yearning wistfully for Thee and harassed by the darkness of the world, am lost? Oh love, in the shape of Arunachala, can the lotus blossom without sight of the sun? Thou art the Sun of suns; Thou causest Grace to well up in abundance and pour forth as a stream!

---

[1] Cf. *The Marital Garland of Letters*, v. 14.

[2] Kama is Cupid; his temptation of Shiva while engaged in *tapas*, ended in his conflagration by a wrathful glance from Shiva's third eye. Out of pity for his disconsolate wife, Rati, Shiva subsequently granted him continued existence in a subtle body.

[3] *Jaganmaya* is universal illusion.

2. Arunachala, Thou Form of Grace Itself! once having claimed me, loveless though I be, how canst Thou let me now be lost, and fail to fill me so with Love that I must pine for Thee unceasingly and melt within like wax over the fire? Oh Nectar springing up in the heart of devotees! Haven of my refuge! Let Thy pleasure be mine, for that way lies my joy, Lord of my life!

3. Drawing me with the cords of Thy Grace, although I had not even dimly thought of Thee, Thou didst decide to kill me outright. How then has one so weak as I offended Thee that Thou dost leave the task unfinished?[1] Why dost Thou torture me thus, keeping me suspended between life and death? Oh Arunachala! fulfil Thy wish, and long survive me all alone, Oh Lord!

4. What did it profit Thee to choose out me from all those struggling in *samsara*,[2] to rescue my helpless self from being lost and hold me at Thy Feet? Lord of the Ocean of Grace! Even to think of Thee puts me to shame. (Long) mayst Thou live! I bow my head to Thee and bless Thee!

5. Lord! Thou didst capture me by stealth and all these days hast held me at Thy Feet! Lord! Thou hast made me (to stand) with hanging head, (dumb) like an image when asked what is Thy nature.[3] Lord! deign to ease me in my weariness, struggling like a deer that is trapped. Lord Arunachala! what can be Thy will? (Yet) who am I to comprehend Thee?

6. Lord of my Life! I am ever at Thy Feet, like a frog (which clings) to the stem of the lotus; make me instead a honey-bee which (from the blossom of the Heart) sucks the sweet honey of Pure Consciousness; then shall I have Deliverance. If I am lost while clinging to Thy Lotus Feet, it will be for Thee a standing column of ignominy, Oh Blazing Pillar of Light, called Arunachala! Oh (wide) Expanse of Grace, more subtle than the ether!

7. Oh Pure One! if the five elements, the living beings and every manifest thing is nothing but Thy all-embracing Light, how then can I (alone) be separate from Thee? Since Thou shinest in the Heart, a single Expanse without duality, how then can I come forth distinct

---

[1] *Alternatively:* What austerities left incomplete (in previous births) have won me Thy special favour? (Cf. *The Marital Garland of Letters*, v. 25 b). What more is left for me to gain or to fulfil?

[2] *Samsara* is the universal flux of manifestation.

[3] *Alternatively:* Thou has made me (rest tense) like a bent bow when asked what is Thy nature.

therefrom? Show Thyself planting Thy Lotus Feet upon the head of the ego as it emerges!

8. Thou has withheld from me all knowledge of gradual attainment while living in the world, and set me at peace; such care indeed is blissful and not painful to anyone, for death in life is in truth glorious.[1] Grant me, wasteful and mad (for Thee), the sovereign remedy of clinging to Thy Feet!

9. O Transcendent! I am the first of those who have not the Supreme Wisdom to clasp Thy Feet in freedom from attachment. Ordain Thou that my burden be transferred to Thee and my free will effaced, for what indeed can be a burden to the Sustainer (of the universe)? Lord Supreme! I have had enough (of the fruits) of carrying (the burden of) this world upon my head, parted from Thee. Arunachala, Supreme Self! think no more to keep me at a distance from Thy Feet!

10. I have discovered a New Thing! This Hill, the Lodestone of lives, arrests the movements of anyone who so much as thinks of it, draws him face to face with It, and fixes him motionless like Itself, to feed upon his soul thus ripened. What (a wonder) is this! Oh souls! beware of It and live![2] Such a destroyer of lives is this magnificent Arunachala, which shines within the Heart!

11. How many are there who have been ruined like me for thinking this Hill to be the Supreme?[3] Oh men who, disgusted with this life of intense misery, seek a means of giving up the body, there is on earth a rare drug which, without actually killing him, will annihilate anyone who so much as thinks of It. Know that It is none other than this Arunachala!

[1] *Alternatively:* Thou has destroyed my ability to earn my living in the world and made a wastrel of me; this condition is miserable and unhappy; to die is better than to live in such ignominy.

[2] *Alternatively:* O souls! think upon It and be saved!

[3] *Alternatively:* How many are there who have lost (their ego) for having thought this Hill to be the Supreme?

SRI ARUNACHALA ASHTAKAM

'The Hill which draws to Itself those who are rich in *jnana-tapas*[1] is this Arunachala.'

(From *Annamalai Venba*, by Guru Namashivaya, disciple of Guha Namashivaya.)

1. Hearken; It stands as an insentient[2] Hill. Its action is mysterious, past human understanding. From the age of innocence it had shone within my mind that Arunachala was something of surpassing grandeur,[3] but even when I came to know through another that it was the same as Tiruvannamalai I did not realize its meaning. When it drew me up to it, stilling my mind, and I came close, I saw it (stand) unmoving.[4]

2. 'Who is the seer?' When I sought within, I watched the disappearance of the seer and what survived him. No thought of 'I saw' arose; how then could the thought 'I did not see' arise? Who has the power to convey this in words, when even Thou (appearing as Dakshinamurty) couldst do so in ancient days by silence only? Only to convey by silence Thy (Transcendent) State Thou standest as a Hill, shining from heaven to earth.

3. When I approach, regarding Thee as having form, Thou standest as a Hill on earth. If (with the mind, the seeker) looks for Thy (essential) form as formless, he is like one who travels the earth to see the (ever-present) ether. To dwell without thought upon Thy (boundless) nature is to lose one's (separate) identity like a doll of

---

[1] i.e. those who are ever intent on gaining wisdom.
[2] The adjective also bears the meaning 'eradicating (objective) knowledge'.
[3] 'To view Chidambaram, to be born in Tiruvarur, to die in Benares, or merely to think of Arunachala is to be assured of Liberation.' This couplet is commonly known in the Brahmin households of South India.
[4] *Alternatively:* I realized that It meant Absolute Stillness.

sugar when it comes in contact with the ocean (of nectar; and) when I come to realize who I am, what else is this identity of mine (but Thee), O Thou Who standest as the towering Aruna Hill?

4. To look for God while ignoring Thee who art Being and Consciousness is like going with a lamp to look for darkness. Only to make Thyself known as Being and Consciousness, Thou dwellest in different religions under different (names and) forms. If (yet) men do not (come) to know Thee, they are indeed the blind who do not know the Sun. Oh Arunachala the Great, Thou peerless Gem, abide and shine Thou as my Self, One without a second!

5. As the string in (a necklet of) gems, it is Thou in Thy Unity who penetratest all the diversity of beings and religions. If, like a gem when it is cut and polished, the (impure) mind is worked against the wheel of the (pure) mind to free it of its flaws, it will take on the light of Thy Grace (and shine) like a ruby, whose fire is unaffected by any outward object. When a sensitive plate has been exposed to the Sun, can it receive impressions afterwards? Oh benign and dazzling Aruna Hill! is there anything apart from Thee?

6. Thou art Thyself the One Being, ever aware as the self-luminous Heart! In Thee there is a mysterious Power (*Shakti*) which without Thee is nothing. From it proceeds the phantom of the mind emitting its latent subtle dark mists, which, illumined by Thy Light (of Consciousness) reflected on them, appear within as thoughts whirling in the vortices of *prarabdha*, later developing into the psychic worlds and projected outwardly as the material world transformed into concrete objects which are magnified by the out-going senses and move about like pictures in a cinema show. Visible or invisible, O Hill of Grace, without Thee they are nothing!

7. Until there is the I-thought, there will be no other thought. Until other thoughts arise, (asking) 'To whom?' (will call forth the reply) 'To me'. He who pursues this closely, questioning 'What is the origin of the I?' and diving inwards reaches the seat of the mind (within) the Heart becomes (there) the Sovereign Lord of the Universe.[1] O boundless Ocean of Grace and Effulgence called Arunachala, dancing motionless within the court of the Heart! there there is no (longer any) dream of such dualities as in and out, right and wrong, birth and death, pleasure and pain, or light and darkness.

---

[1] *Literally:* The Sovereign Lord under the shade of a single umbrella.

8. The waters rise up from the sea as clouds, then fall as rain and run back to the sea in streams; nothing can keep them from returning to their source. Likewise the soul rising up from Thee cannot be kept from joining Thee again, although it turns in many eddies on its way. A bird which rises from the earth and soars into the sky can find no place of rest in mid-air, but must return again to earth. So indeed must all retrace their path, and when the soul finds the way back to its source, it will sink and be merged in Thee, O Arunachala, Thou Ocean of Bliss!

SRI ARUNACHALA PANCHARATNA

FIVE STANZAS TO SRI ARUNACHALA

Ocean of Nectar, full of Grace, engulfing the universe in Thy Splendour! Oh Arunachala, the Supreme Itself! be Thou the Sun and open the lotus of my heart in Bliss!

This is the opening stanza of the Pancharatna which in the form of a *stotra* (praise of God) contains the gist of Supreme Knowledge born of Realization. It is said to be like *sutras*, very terse with much deeper significance than appears superficially.

Arunachala—*Aruna* (Light) plus *Achala* (mountain), means the *Tejolingam* (symbol of light) of Siva. Its significance for the individual is that when one gets beyond body-consciousness, the inner Self shines pure and clear.

Ordinary loss of body-consciousness, as in shocks, results only in darkness, whereas the same brought about voluntarily for the purpose of Self-Realization, ends in the Illumination of the Self, by the sole Grace of God.

Such illumination destroys the ego, producing complete self-surrender to the Lord. The Lord is Eternal; the sense of Eternity is Bliss (Nectar).

Just as the lotus bud, flourishing in marshy pools, blossoms at sunrise, so also the heart, behind the soiled mind, shines forth by the Grace of God who is the Self of all selves and who is externally visible as Arunachala. But this sun, after rising up, never sets again and the Heart of the Realized Soul is in blossom once and for all.

Oh Arunachala! in Thee the picture of the universe is formed, has its stay, and is dissolved; this is the sublime Truth. Thou art the Inner Self, Who dancest in the Heart as 'I'. 'Heart' is Thy name, Oh Lord!

This sloka refers to God first as Creator, Preserver, and Destroyer, and then as realized by the Enlightened.

The Liberated say that just as God is the stay of the universe, so also, the Heart is of the individual. The part must be of the nature of the whole; the Whole (God) is Infinity. Therefore, there is no distinction between the Heart and God.

God is consciousness, as also is the Heart. Self-contained and sublime, it manifests as the individual self concomitantly with an individualizing force perceptible as the 'ego' or 'I'. If the ego is traced back, they say that there becomes perceptible a vibration from the Heart, signifying the Real Self.

He who turns inward with untroubled mind to search where the consciousness of 'I' arises, realizes the Self, and rests in Thee, Oh Arunachala! like a river when it joins the ocean.

This sloka deals with *Jnana marga*, the Path of Knowledge, followed by enquirers and seekers after Truth. It is one of the three or even four Paths to Realization of Self. These are *Jnana*, Yoga, *Bhakti*, and *Karma*.

The ocean, being the store of all waters, evaporates, clouds are formed, and rain falls, giving rise to rivers which as soon as formed become restless, as it were, course along as if to find their origin and repose only after being discharged into the ocean. Similarly, the individual emanating from the Heart is restless, and becomes eager to find his own source. The way is the trail of the 'ego' into the Heart.

Abandoning the outer world, with mind and breath controlled, to meditate on Thee within, the Yogi sees Thy Light, Oh Arunachala! and finds his delight in Thee.

This stanza deals with Yoga *marga*, described in Patanjali's 'Yoga Sutras'.

While a *Jnani* seeks within for the source of the ego and is liberated on tracing it to the Heart, a *Yogi*, craving to see the Glory of God, turns away from other pursuits and concentrates on Him (in the shape or name of Arunachala). The Hill, though material in outward appearance, becomes full of life, and perceptible in the transcendental vision of the Yogi, as the Universal Glorious Light, the same as the Self.

He who dedicates his mind to Thee and, seeing Thee, always beholds the universe as Thy figure, he who at all times glorifies Thee and loves Thee as none other than the Self, he is the master without rival, being one with Thee, Oh Arunachala! and lost in Thy Bliss.

The first part of this stanza deals with *bhakti marga*. Glorifying God with intense love, one passes beyond *samsara* and is happy at being merged in Him. This is *bhakti*. The transcendental vision reveals Arunachala as one's own Master, and such repeated experiences convince one of the Immanence of God. Complete surrender of Self ensues and what remains over is only the all-pervading, and ever-present, Glorious Being-Consciousness. Transcendence sweeps away names and forms and the result is Infinity, Eternity.

The second part of the stanza deals with *karma marga*. Feeling God's immanence everywhere, one considers oneself not as the agent, but as a tool to serve God in the shape of one's surroundings.

There are three aspects of God according to one's own realization. They are:

Sat (Being), *Chit* (Consciousness), *Ananda* (Bliss).

The *Sat* aspect is emphasized by *jnanis* who are said to repose in the Essence of Being after incessant search for the same and with their individuality lost in the Supreme.

The *Chit* aspect is for yogis who exert themselves to control their breath in order to steady the mind and are then said to see the Glory (consciousness of Being) of God as the One light radiating in all directions.

The *Ananda* aspect is for devotees who become intoxicated with the nectar of the love of God and lose themselves in Blissful experience. Unwilling to leave this, they remain for ever merged in God.

The four *margas*, *Karma*, *Bhakti*, Yoga, and *Jnana*, are not exclusive of one another. Each is however described separately in classical works only to convey an idea of the appropriate aspect of God to appeal readily to the aspirant according to his predisposition. This *stotra*, though short, is compact and can be so expanded as to be of interest also to scholars and philosophers.

4

Forty Verses

ONE of the devotees of Bhagavan was the outstanding Tamil poet Muruganar. He importuned Bhagavan for a cycle of forty verses giving a succinct synopsis of his teaching. Bhagavan wrote the verses as occasion arose, and when there were the required number Muruganar took them and arranged them in continuous form. Later a supplement consisting of a second forty verses was added. So indifferent to authorship was Bhagavan that he did not write all these supplementary verses himself. When he came upon a suitable one he used it, mostly translating from Sanskrit, and when not he made one. In this volume those verses which he took from older sources are printed in italics.

These eighty verses are the most comprehensive exposition of the Maharshi's teaching. A number of translations have been made and commentaries written on them. They have been published as a separate booklet by the Asramam under the titles 'Ulladu Narpadu', 'Sad-Vidya' and 'Truth Revealed'.

*   *   *   *   *

INVOCATORY

i. If Reality did not exist, could there be any knowledge of existence? Free from all thoughts, Reality abides in the Heart, the Source of all thoughts. It is, therefore, called the Heart. How then is one to contemplate it? To be as It is in the Heart, is Its contemplation.

ii. Those who know intense fear of death seek refuge only at the feet of the Lord Who has neither death nor birth. Dead to themselves and their possessions, can the thought of death occur to them again? Deathless are they.

*　　　*　　　*　　　*　　　*

1. From our perception of the world there follows acceptance of a unique First Principle possessing various powers. Pictures of name and form, the person who sees, the screen on which he sees, and the light by which he sees: he himself is all of these.

2. All religions postulate the three fundamentals, the world, the soul, and God, but it is only the one Reality that manifests Itself as these three. One can say 'The three are really three' only so long as the ego lasts. Therefore, to inhere in one's own Being, where the 'I', or ego, is dead, is the perfect State.

3. 'The world is real.' 'No, it is a mere illusory appearance.' 'The world is conscious.' 'No.' 'The world is happiness.' 'No.' What use is it to argue thus? That State is agreeable to all, wherein, having given up the objective outlook, one knows one's Self and loses all notions either of unity or duality, of oneself and the ego.

4. If one has form oneself, the world and God also will appear to have form, but if one is formless, who is it that sees those forms, and how? Without the eye can any object be seen? The seeing Self is the Eye, and that Eye is the Eye of Infinity.

5. The body is a form composed of the five-fold sheath; therefore, all the five sheaths are implied in the term 'body'. Apart from the body does the world exist? Has anyone seen the world without the body?

6. The world is nothing more than an embodiment of the objects perceived by the five sense-organs. Since, through these five sense-organs, a single mind perceives the world, the world is nothing but the mind. Apart from the mind can there be a world?

7. Although the world and knowledge thereof rise and set together it is by knowledge alone that the world is made apparent. That Perfection, wherein the world and knowledge thereof rise and set, and which shines without rising and setting, is alone the Reality.

8. Under whatever name and form one may worship the Absolute Reality, it is only a means for realizing It without name and form. That alone is true realization, wherein one knows oneself in

relation to that Reality, attains peace and realizes one's identity with It.

9. The duality of subject and object and the trinity of seer, sight, and seen can exist only if supported by the One. If one turns inward in search of that One Reality they fall away. Those who see this are those who see Wisdom. They are never in doubt.

10. Ordinary knowledge is always accompanied by ignorance, and ignorance by knowledge; the only true Knowledge is that by which one knows the Self through enquiring as to whose is the knowledge and ignorance.

11. Is it not, rather, ignorance to know all else without knowing oneself, the knower? As soon as one knows the Self, which is the substratum of knowledge and ignorance, knowledge and ignorance perish.

12. That alone is true Knowledge which is neither knowledge nor ignorance. What is known is not true Knowledge. Since the Self shines with nothing else to know or to make known, It alone is Knowledge. It is not a void.

13. The Self, which is Knowledge, is the only Reality. Knowledge of multiplicity is false knowledge. This false knowledge, which is really ignorance, cannot exist apart from the Self, which is Knowledge-Reality. The variety of gold ornaments is unreal, since none of them can exist without the gold of which they are all made.

14. If the first person, I, exists, then the second and third persons, you and he, will also exist. By enquiring into the nature of the I, the I perishes. With it you and he also perish. The resultant state, which shines as Absolute Being, is one's own natural state, the Self.

15. Only with reference to the present can the past and the future exist. They too, while current, are the present. To try to determine the nature of the past and the future while ignoring the present is like trying to count without the unit.

61. Apart from us where is time and where is space? If we are bodies, we are involved in time and space, but are we? We are one and identical now, then, and forever, here, there, and everywhere. Therefore we, timeless and spaceless Being, alone are.

17. To those who have not realized the Self, as well as to those who have, the word 'I 'refers to the body, but with this difference, that for those who have not realized, the 'I' is confined to the body

whereas for those who have realized the Self within the body the 'I' shines as the limitless Self.

18. To those who have not realized (the Self) as well as to those who have realized, the world is real. But to those who have not realized, Truth is adapted to the measure of the world, whereas to those that have realized, Truth shines as the Formless Perfection, and as the Substratum of the world. This is all the difference between them.

19. Only those who have no knowledge of the Source of destiny and free will dispute as to which of them prevails. They that know the Self as the one Source of destiny and free will are free from both. Will they again get entangled in them?

20. He who sees God without seeing the Self sees only a mental image. They say that he who sees the Self sees God. He who, having completely lost the ego, sees the Self, has found God, because the Self does not exist apart from God.

21. What is the Truth of the scriptures which declare that if one sees the Self one sees God? How can one see one's Self? If, since one is a single being, one cannot see one's Self, how can one see God? Only by becoming a prey to Him.

22. The Divine gives light to the mind and shines within it. Except by turning the mind inward and fixing it in the Divine, there is no other way to know Him through the mind.

23. The body does not say 'I'. No one will argue that even in deep sleep the 'I' ceases to exist. Once the 'I' emerges, all else emerges. With a keen mind enquire whence this 'I' emerges.

24. This inert body does not say 'I'. Reality-Consciousness does not emerge. Between the two, and limited to the measure of the body, something emerges as 'I'. It is this that is known as *Chit-jada-granthi* (the knot between the Conscious and the inert), and also as bondage, soul, subtle body, ego, *samsara*, mind, and so forth.

25. It comes into being equipped with a form, and as long as it retains a form it endures. Having a form, it feeds and grows big. But if you investigate it this evil Spirit, which has no form of its own, relinquishes its grip on form and takes to flight.

26. If the ego is, everything else also is. If the ego is not, nothing else is. Indeed, the ego is all. Therefore the enquiry as to what this ego is, is the only way of giving up everything.

27. The State of non-emergence of 'I' is the state of being THAT. Without questing for that State of the non-emergence of 'I' and attaining It, how can one accomplish one's own extinction, from which the 'I' does not revive? Without that attainment how is it possible to abide in one's true State, where one is THAT?

28. Just as a man would dive in order to get something that had fallen into the water, so one should dive into oneself, with a keen one-pointed mind, controlling speech and breath, and find the place whence the 'I' originates.

29. The only enquiry leading to Self-realization is seeking the Source of the 'I' with in-turned mind and without uttering the word 'I'. Meditation on 'I am not this; I am That' may be an aid to the enquiry but it cannot be the enquiry.

30. If one enquires 'Who am I?' within the mind, the individual 'I' falls down abashed as soon as one reaches the Heart and immediately Reality manifests itself spontaneously as 'I-I'. Although it reveals itself as 'I', it is not the ego but the Perfect Being, the Absolute Self.

31. For Him who is immersed in the bliss of the Self, arising from the extinction of the ego, what remains to be accomplished? He is not aware of anything (as) other than the Self. Who can apprehend his State?

32. Although the scriptures proclaim 'Thou art That', it is only a sign of weakness of mind to meditate 'I am That, not this', because you are eternally That. What has to be done is to investigate what one really is and remain That.

33. It is ridiculous to say either 'I have not realized the Self' or 'I have realized the Self'; are there two selves, for one to be the object of the other's realization? It is a truth within the experience of everyone that there is only one Self.

34. It is due to illusion born of ignorance that men fail to recognize That which is always and for everybody the inherent Reality dwelling in its natural Heart-centre and to abide in it, and that instead they argue that it exists or does not exist, that it has form or has not form, or is non-dual or dual.

35. To seek and abide in the Reality that is always attained is the only Attainment. All other attainments (*siddhis*) are such as are acquired in dreams. Can they appear real to someone who has woken

up from sleep? Can they that are established in the Reality and are free from *maya*, be deluded by them?

36. Only if the thought 'I am the body' occurs will the meditation 'I am not this, I am That' help one to abide as That. Why should we for ever be thinking, 'I am That'? Is it necessary for man to go on thinking 'I am a man'? Are we not always That?

37. The contention 'Dualism during practice, non-dualism on Attainment' is also false. While one is anxiously searching, as well as when one has found one's Self, who else is one but the tenth man?[1]

38. As long as a man is the doer, he also reaps the fruit of his deeds, but as soon as he realizes the Self through enquiry as to who is the doer his sense of being the doer falls away and the triple *karma* is ended. This is the state of eternal Liberation.

39. Only so long as one considers oneself bound, do thoughts of bondage and Liberation continue. When one enquires who is bound the Self is realized, eternally attained, and eternally free. When thought of bondage comes to an end, can thought of Liberation survive?

40. If it is said that Liberation is of three kinds, with form or without form or with and without form, then let me tell you that the extinction of the three forms of Liberation is the only true Liberation.

[1] This refers to a traditional story of a party of ten fools who were travelling together They had to cross a river and on reaching the other shore wanted to check up whether all of them had got safely across. Each one counted in turn, but each one counted the nine others and forgot himself. So they thought the tenth man had been drowned and began to mourn him. Just then a traveller came past and asked them what was the matter. He at once saw the cause of their mistake and in order to convince them he made them walk past him one by one, giving each one a blow as he passed and telling them to count the strokes.

SUPPLEMENT TO THE FORTY VERSES

'THAT in which all these worlds are fixed, of which they are, from which they arise, for which they exist, because of which they come into being, and which they really are—THAT alone is the Real, the Truth. That is the Treasure in the Heart.[1]

1. *Association with Sages who have realized the Truth removes material attachments; on these attachments being removed the attachments of the mind are also destroyed. Those whose attachments of mind are thus destroyed become one with That which is Motionless. They attain Liberation while yet alive. Cherish association with such Sages.*

2. *That Supreme State which is obtained here and now as a result of association with Sages, and realized through the deep meditation of Self-enquiry in contact with the Heart, cannot be gained with the aid of a Guru or through knowledge of the scriptures, or by spiritual merit, or by any other means.*

3. *If association with Sages is obtained, to what purpose are the various methods of self-discipline? Tell me, of what use is a fan when the cool, gentle, south wind is blowing?*

4. *The heat of mental and bodily excitement is allayed by (the rays of) the moon; want and misery are removed by the* kalpaka *tree;[2] sins are washed away by the sacred waters of the Ganges. All these afflictions are altogether banished by the mere* darshan *of the peerless Sage.*

5. *Neither the holy waters of pilgrimage, nor the images of gods made of earth and stone, can stand comparison with the benign look of the Sage. They make one pure only after countless days of grace, but no sooner does the Sage bestow his gracious glance than he makes one pure!*

6. *Disciple: Who is God?*
   Master: He who knows the mind.

---

[1] *Alternatively:* May we adore That at Heart.
[2] The celestial tree that grants all the boons one prays for.

D: My mind is known by me, the Spirit.

M: Since the Srutis *declare, 'God is only One', you (as the knower of the mind) are really God.*

7. *Master: What is the light for you?*

Disciple: By day the sun; by night, a lamp.

M: What is the light that perceives that light?

D: The eye.

M: What is the light that illumines the eye?

D: That light is the intellect.

M: What is the Light that knows the intellect?

D: It is the 'I'.

M: You are (therefore) the supreme Light of (all) lights.

D: That am I.

8. In the interior of the Heart-cave there shines alone the One Brahman as 'I-I', the self-conscious Atman. Realize that State of steadfast inherence in the Self, entering into the Heart either by diving deep within through Self-enquiry or by the submergence of the mind through breath-control.

9. *Know that the pure and changeless Self-awareness in the Heart is the Knowledge which, through the destruction of the ego, bestows Liberation.*

10. The body is inert like an earthen pot. Since it has no I-consciousness and since in deep sleep, when bodiless,[1] we experience our natural being, the body cannot be the I. Who then is it that causes I-ness? Whence is he? In the Heart-cave of those who thus enquire and who know and abide as the Self, Lord Arunachala Siva shines forth of Himself as the 'That-am-I' Consciousness.

11. Who is born? Know that he alone is born who, enquiring 'Whence am I born?' is born in the Source of his being. The Supreme Sage is he, eternally born, again and again, day after day.

12. Cast off the notion 'I-am-the-contemptible-body'. Ponder over and realize the Self of perennial bliss. *Seeking to know the Self while cherishing the body is like getting hold of a crocodile as a raft to cross a river.*

13. Charity, Penance, Sacrifice, Duty, Yoga, Devotion, the Expanse of Consciousness, the Substance, Peace, the Truth, Grace, Silence, the supreme State, the deathless Death, Knowledge,

[1] i.e. when there is no bodily awareness.

Renunciation, Liberation, and Bliss, know that all these are synonymous with the severance of the 'I am-the-body' Consciousness.

14. The only path of *karma*, *bhakti*, yoga, and *jnana* is to enquire who it is who has *karma* (action), *vibhakti* (lack of devotion), *viyoga* (separation) and *ajnana* (ignorance). Through this investigation the ego disappears and the state of abidance in the Self, in which none of these negative qualities ever existed, remains as the Truth.

15. There are some foolish persons who, not realizing that they themselves are moved by the Divine Power, seek to attain all the supernatural powers of action. They are like the lame man who said: 'I can dispose of the enemy if someone will hold me up on my legs.'

16. Since peace of mind is permanent in Liberation, how can they who yoke their mind to powers—which are unattainable except through the activity of the mind—become merged in the Bliss of Liberation which subdues the agitation of the mind?

17. The Lord bears the burden of the world. Know that the spurious ego which presumes to bear that burden is like a sculptured figure at the foot of a temple tower which appears to sustain the tower's weight. Whose fault is it if the traveller, instead of putting his luggage in the cart which bears the load anyway, carries it on his head, to his own incovenience?

18. *Between the two breasts, below the chest and above the abdomen, there are six viscera of various colours. Of these one resembles a lily bud and is two digits to the right of centre. This is the Heart.*[1]

19. *It is inverted, and in it there is a tiny orifice wherein is firmly seated along with latent tendencies etc. an immense darkness. Thereon the entire nervous system has its support. It is the seat of the vital forces, the mind, and the light of consciousness.*

20. *That Divinity which shines as the 'I' in the cavity of the Heart-lotus is adored as the Lord Guhesa. When, through intensive practice, the bhavana*[2] *'He am I', that is 'That Guhesa am I', is as firmly established as the 'I'-notion deep-rooted in your body, and when you abide ever as that Divinity itself, It shines forth, whereupon ignorance, that is the notion 'I-am-the-perishable-body', is dispelled like darkness before the rising sun.*

---

[1] This does not refer to the muscular organ on the left but to the spiritual Heart-Centre at the right side of the chest.

[2] *Bhavana* consists in being attuned to That.

21. 'Tell me what it is that is described as the Heart of all the individuals of the world, in which (as in a) big mirror all this universe is perceived as a reflection,' Rama once asked the Sage Vasishta, and the latter replied: 'After investigation (it has been declared that) the Heart for all individuals is twofold.

22. 'Listen and understand the characteristics of the two, the one to be accepted and the other to be rejected. That organ which is called the heart and is situated at a particular spot within the chest of the physical body is to be rejected. That Heart which is of the form of Absolute Knowledge is to be accepted. Though it is both within and without, it is devoid of an inner and an outer side.

23. 'That alone is the Supreme Heart, and in it all this world abides. It is the mirror of all objects, and the abode of all wealth. Hence, for all living beings that Knowledge alone is declared to be the Heart. It is not a part of the perishable body which is insentient like a stone.

24. 'Therefore the destruction of the latent tendencies of the mind comes about spontaneously as the result of earnest endeavour to hold the ego in the Heart of perfect purity and absolute Knowledge, together with breath-control!

25. 'Ever abiding in the Heart through the incessant meditation, "I am that Lord Siva, who is Pure Knowledge, free from all qualitative limitations," remove all attachments of the ego.

26. 'Having investigated the three states (waking, dream, and deep sleep) and holding steadfastly in your heart to the Supreme State which is above them and is free from illusion, play your part in the world, Oh hero Raghava! You have realized in the heart That which is the Substratum of Reality beneath all appearances. Therefore without ever abandoning that viewpoint, play your part in the world as you please.

27. 'As one with feigned enthusiasm and joy, with feigned excitement and hatred, as one taking feigned initiative and, making a feigned effort, play your part in the world, Oh hero Raghava!'

28. He who has conquered the senses through Wisdom is the only true Jnani established in Self-knowledge. Proclaim him to be the Fire of Knowledge, the wielder of the Thunderbolt of Knowledge, Death unto death, and the Hero who has killed death.

29. Know that (the qualities of) lustre, intelligence, and strength develop of themselves in those who have realized the Truth, (just as)

the quality of beauty and all other attractive features embellish nature with the advent of spring.

30. *The mind which is free from latent tendencies is not really engaged in activity even though it performs actions, just as people who hear a story while their mind wanders elsewhere (do not really listen). The mind which is immersed in latent tendencies is really engaged in activity even though it does not perform actions, like a person who, in a dream, climbs a hill and falls down a precipice, although his body stays motionless.*

31. To the Jnani, who is asleep in the gross body, the states of activity, *samadhi*, and sleep mean no more than a cart's moving, stopping, and being yoked mean to a traveller who is asleep in it.

32. The Fourth State, which is beyond the three States, is the only Reality. It is known as the transcendent state of waking sleep. Since the three apparent states do not really exist, know that the Fourth is transcendent.

33. To say that *sanchita* (karma accumulated in the past, to be worked out in this life) and *agami* (karma to be worked out in future lives) do not adhere to the *Jnani*, but that *prarabdha* (karma being worked out in the present life) does, is merely a formal reply to the query put by others. Know that just as after the death of the husband none of his wives can remain unwidowed, so after the destruction of the doer none of the three karmas can remain.

34. *For men of little understanding wife, children, and others comprise the family. Know that for the learned there is a family made up of countless books in their mind which is an obstacle to yoga.*

35. What use is the learning of those who do not seek to wipe out the letters of destiny[1] by enquiring 'Whence is the birth of us who know the letters?' They have sunk to the level of a gramophone. What else are they, O Arunachala!

36. It is those who are not learned that are saved rather than those whose ego has not yet subsided in spite of their learning. The unlearned are saved from the unrelenting grip of the devil of self-infatuation; they are saved from the malady of a myriad whirling thoughts and words; they are saved from running after wealth. It is from more than one evil that they are saved.

---

[1] This refers to the conception of the letters of a man's destiny written on his forehead. To wipe out the letters is to transcend one's destiny or *karma*.

37. *Although he may renounce the whole world and acquire all knowledge, it is rare indeed for one to be saved who has sunk into subjection to the vile prostitute flattery.*

38. Who is there apart from the Self, if one only abides ever as the Self, without swerving from that primal State and never differentiating oneself from others? What does it matter if others say anything about oneself? What indeed does it matter if it is oneself alone that one praises or abuses?

39. *Retain at heart the sense of non-duality but never express it in action. O my son, the sense of non-duality may apply to the three worlds, but know that in relation to the Master it will never do.*

40. *I will proclaim in truth the quintessence of the established conclusions of the entire Vedanta. It is that when the ego is destroyed it becomes That and then the Self in the form of Absolute Consciousness alone remains.*

5

Upadesa Saram

THE ESSENCE OF INSTRUCTION

THERE is an old legend that a group of Rishis once lived in the forest together, practising rites by which they acquired supernatural powers. By the same means they hoped to attain final Liberation. In this, however, they were mistaken, for action can only result in action; not in the cessation of action; rites can produce powers but not the Peace of Liberation which is beyond rites and powers and all forms of action. Siva determined to convince them of their error and therefore appeared before them as a wandering sadhu. Together with him came Vishnu in the form of a beautiful lady. All the Rishis were smitten with love for this lady and thereby their equilibrium was disturbed and their rites and powers were adversely affected. Moreover their wives, who were also living with them in the forest, all fell in love with the strange sadhu. Incensed at this, they conjured up an elephant and a tiger by magic rites and sent them against him. Siva, however, slew them easily and took the elephant's skin for a robe and the tiger's for a wrap. The Rishis then realized that they were up against one more powerful than themselves and they bowed down to him and asked him for instruction. He then explained to them that it is not by action but by renunciation of action that one attains to Liberation.

The poet Muruganar was writing this legend in Tamil verse, but when he came to the instruction given to the Rishis by Siva he asked Bhagavan, who was Siva Incarnate, to write it for him. Bhagavan accordingly wrote the instruction in thirty Tamil verses. He himself later translated these into Sanskrit, and the Sanskrit version was daily chanted before him together with the Vedas and continues to be chanted before his shrine; that is to say that it is treated as a scripture. He refers to the various paths to Liberation, grading them in order of efficiency and excellence, and showing that the best is Self-enquiry.

*   *   *   *   *

1. Action (karma) bears fruit (in action), for so the Creator ordains. But is it God? (It cannot be for) it is not sentient.

2. The results of action pass away, and yet leave seeds that cast the agent into an ocean of action. Action (therefore) does not bring Liberation.

3. But acts performed without any attachment, in the spirit of service to God, cleanse the mind and point the way to Liberation.

4. This is certain: worship, incantations, and meditation are performed respectively with the body, the voice, and the mind and are in this ascending order of value.

5. One can regard this eightfold[1] universe as a manifestation of God; and whatever worship is performed in it is excellent as the worship of God.

6. The repetition aloud of His name is better than praise. Better still is its faint murmur. But the best is repetition within the mind— and that is meditation, above referred to.

7. Better than such broken thought (meditation) is its steady and continuous flow like the flow of oil or of a perennial stream.

8. The lofty attitude 'He am I' is preferable to the attitude 'He is not me'.

9. Remaining in the Real Being, transcending all thought, through intense devotion, is the very essence of Supreme *Bhakti*.

10. 'Absorption into the source' or core of Existence (or the Heart) is what the paths of Karma, *Bhakti*, Yoga, and *Jnana* teach.

11. As birds are caught with nets, so by holding the breath, the mind is restrained and absorbed. This (breath-regulation) is a device for effecting absorption.

12. For mind and life-breath (*prana*), expressed in thought and action, diverge and branch out, but they spring from a single root.

13. Absorption has two forms, *laya* and *nasha*. That which is merely absorbed in *laya* revives; if it is dead, it does not revive.

14. When the mind gets absorbed by breath-restraint, then it will 'die', (i.e. its form will perish) if fixed to a single point.

[1] Eightfold in that it is composed of the five elements, the sun and moon and the individual being.

15. The great yogi whose mind is extinguished and who rests in Brahman, has no karma, as he has attained his true nature (Brahman).

16. When the mind withdraws from external objects of sense and beholds (i.e. engages in mystic introspection of) its own effulgent form, that is true wisdom.

17. When the mind unceasingly investigates its own nature, it transpires that there is no such thing as mind. This is the direct path for all.

18. The mind is merely thoughts. Of all thoughts, the thought 'I' is the root. (Therefore) the mind is only the thought 'I'.

19. 'Whence does this "I" arise?' Seek for it within; it then vanishes. This is the pursuit of Wisdom.

20. Where the 'I' vanished, there appears an 'I-I' by itself. This is the Infinite (*Purnam*).

21. This is always the true import of the term 'I'. For we do not cease to exist even in the deepest sleep, where there is no waking 'I'.

22. The body, senses, mind, life-breath (*prana*), and ignorance (*avidya* or *sushupti*) are all insentient and not the Real. I am the Real (*Sat*). These (sheaths) I am not.

23. As there is no second being to know that which is, 'that which is' is conscious. We are that.

24. Creatures and Creator both exist. They are One in Being. Their differences are the degrees of their knowledge and other attributes.

25. When the creature sees and knows himself without attributes, that is knowledge of the Creator, for the Creator appears as no other than the Self.

26. To know the Self is to be the Self—as there are not two separate selves. This (state) is *thanmaya nishta* (abiding as That).

27. That is real knowledge which transcends both knowledge and ignorance. There is no object to be known There.

28. When one's true nature is known, then there is Being without beginning and end; It is unbroken Awareness-Bliss.

29. Remaining in this state of Supreme Bliss, past all thoughts of bondage and release, is abiding in the service of the Supreme.

30. The Realization of That which subsists when all trace of 'I' is gone, is good *tapas*. So sings Ramana the Self of all.

6

Miscellaneous Verse

THE SONG OF THE *POPPADUM*

DURING the years when Bhagavan was living at Skandas-
ramam, an ashram formed from a cave on Arunachala, that
is from 1914 to 1922, his mother lived there too and did
most of the cooking. He himself was a skilled cook and both now
and later often helped to prepare the food. On one occasion his
mother was making *poppadum*, a thin round cake made of black
gram flour and fried crisp, and she called to him to help her. Instead
of doing so, however, he composed this poem giving instruction
for spiritual development under the symbolism of making *poppadum*.

No need about the world to roam
And suffer from depression;
Make *poppadum* within the home
According to the lesson
Of 'THOU ART THAT', without compare,
The Unique Word,[1] unspoken,
'Tis not by speech it will declare.
The silence is unbroken
Of Him who is the Adept-Sage,
The great Apotheosis,
With His eternal heritage
That Being-Wisdom-Bliss is.

Make *poppadum* and after making fry,
Eat, so your cravings you may satisfy.

[1] i.e. Stillness is paradoxically the speech of the Eternal Spirit.

The grain which is the black gram's yield,
The so-called self or ego,
Grown in the body's fertile field
Of five-fold sheaths,[1] put into
The roller-mill made out of stone,
Which is the search for Wisdom,
The 'Who am I?'. 'Tis thus alone
The Self will gain its freedom.
This must be crushed to finest dust
And ground up into fragments
As being the non-self, so must
We shatter our attachments.

Make *poppadum* . . .

Mix in the juice of square-stemmed vine,
This is association
With Holy Men. With this combine
Within the preparation
Some cummin-seed of mind-control
And pepper of restraining
The wayward senses, with them roll
That salt which is remaining
Indifferent to the world we see,
With condiment of leanings
Towards a virtuous unity.
These are their different meanings.

Make *poppadum* . . .

The mixture into dough now blend
And on the stone then place it
Of mind, by tendencies hardened,
And without ceasing baste it

---

[1] The Hindu philosophical doctrines recognize the existence of subtler bodies of the human being, each functioning in a finer realm. The five sheaths mentioned in the text are included in the three human bodies—material, subtle, and causal. These sheaths are: the physical, vital, mental, intellectual, and blissful sheaths. For a description see the Viveka-chudamani.

With heavy strokes of the 'I-I'
Delivered with the pestle
Of introverted mind. Slowly
The mind will cease to wrestle.
Then roll out with the pin of peace
Upon the slab of Brahman.
Continue effort without cease
With energetic élan.

Make *poppadum* . . .

The *poppadum* or soul's now fit
To put into the fry-pan,
The one infinite symbol it
Of the great Silence, which can
Be first prepared by putting in
Some clarified fresh butter
Of the Supreme. And now begin
To heat it till it sputter,
On Wisdom's self-effulgent flame
Fry *poppadum*, 'I', as That.
Enjoying all alone the same;
Which bliss we ever aim at.

Make *poppadum* of self and after eat;
Of Perfect Peace then you will be replete.

ATMA-VIDYA

SELF-KNOWLEDGE

A devotee once wrote on a slip of paper that Self-knowledge is the easiest thing, since one already is the Self, and handed it to Bhagavan, asking him to write a poem on the subject. This is the poem written.

1. Self-knowledge is an easy thing,
   The easiest thing there is.
   The Self is something that's entirely real
   Even for the most ordinary man,
   It could be said that a clear gooseberry[1]
   Is an illusion by comparison.

2. The Self, which shines as Sun within the Heart,
   Is real and all-pervading. 'Twill reveal
   Itself as soon as false thought is destroyed
   And not one speck remains. For this thought is
   The cause of the appearance of false forms,
   The body and the world, which seem to be
   Real things in spite of Self, which steadfast stands
   The ever-changeless, firm as Truth itself.
   When Self shines forth darkness will be dispersed,
   Affliction cease and Bliss alone remain.

3. The thought 'I am the body' is the string
   On which are threaded divers thoughts like beads.
   Therefore on diving deep upon the quest
   'Who am I and from whence?' thoughts disappear
   And consciousness of Self then flashes forth
   As the 'I-I' within the cavity

---

[1] The fruit mentioned in the Tamil text is the *nelli,* widely grown in India but unknown in Europe. It is more or less transparent and hence "as clear as the nelli in one's hand" is the Tamil equivalent to the English saying: "as clear as crystal".

Of every seeker's Heart. And this is Heaven,
This is that Stillness, the abode of Bliss.

4. What is the use of knowing everything
Except the Self? What else is there to know
For anyone when Self, Itself, is known?
On realizing in oneself the Self,
Which is the only self-effulgent One
In myriads of selves, the Light of Self
Will clearly shine within. This is indeed
The true display of Grace, the ego's death,
And the unfolding of the Bliss Supreme.

5. In order that the bonds of destiny
And all its kindred may at last be loosed,
And so that one may also be released
From the dread cycle of both birth and death,
This path than others is far easier,
Therefore be still and keep a silent hold
On tongue and mind and body. That which is
The Self-effulgent will arise within.
This is the Supreme Experience. Fear will cease.
This is the boundless sea of Perfect Bliss!

6. Annamalai,[1] the Transcendental One,
That is the Eye behind the eye of mind,
Which eye and other senses cognize,
Which in their turn illuminate the Sky,
And all the other elements as well,
That is again the Spirit-sky in which
The mind-sky doth appear, That shines within
The Heart which is of every thought quite free,
And with gaze fixed within remains as That;
Annamalai, the Self-effulgent shines.
But Grace[2] is needed most. So faithful be
Unto the Self and Bliss will then result.

[1] This Tamil name is a word meaning 'insurmountable hill' and is here used to address and signify the Inner Self, which is beyond the reach of thought and word.
[2] i.e. Grace coming from an Adept-Sage is necessary as a prerequisite to obtain such illuminating experience.

VERSES ON THE CELEBRATION OF BHAGAVAN'S BIRTHDAY

Bhagavan's birthday falls in the month of December, but the date by the Western calendar varies according to the phase of the moon. It is at full moon, and, in the year of his birth, 1879, fell on December 29th. It was one of the great annual festivals at his Ashram and still is. When first it was proposed to celebrate it, however, he protested and composed the following poem. He gave in, later, to the importunity of his disciples.

'You who wish to celebrate the birthday, seek first whence was your birth. One's true birthday is when he enters That which transcends birth and death—the Eternal Being.

At least on one's birthday one should mourn one's entry into this world (*samsara*). To glory in it and celebrate it is like delighting in and decorating a corpse. To seek one's Self and merge in the Self: that is wisdom.'

COMPLAINT OF THE STOMACH

One day there had been feasting at the Ashram. Many had been upset by the large quantity of rich food. Someone quoted the following complaint about the stomach by the Tamil poet Avvayar:

* * * * *

'You will not go without food even for one day, nor will you take enough for two days at a time. You have no idea of the trouble I have on your account, Oh wretched stomach! It is impossible to get on with you!'

* * * * *

Bhagavan immediately replied with a parody giving the stomach's complaint against the ego.

* * * * *

'You will not give even an hour's rest to me, your stomach. Day after day, every hour, you keep on eating. You have no idea how I suffer, Oh trouble-making ego! It is impossible to get on with you.'

STRAY VERSES

These verses were written at odd times by Bhagavan and included in some of the poems of Muruganar. The order used here was suggested by Bhagavan.

1. One syllable shines for ever in the heart as Self.
   Who is there anywhere who can write it down?
2. Incantation reaching to the source of sound is the best course for those who are not firm in Consciousness which is the source of the I.
3. This excreta-making body for Self he who mistakes
   Is worse than one who, born a pig, for food excreta takes.
4. Incessant search for Self the love supreme of God we call,
   For He alone as Self abides within the Heart of all.
5. What introverted mind calls Peace outside as power is shown;
   Those who have reached and found this Truth their Unity have known.
6. He who's contented with his lot, from jealousy is free;
   Balanced in affluence and mishap; not bound by action he.
7. By him alone who's saved himself can other folk be freed;
   The help of others is as if the blind the blind would lead.
8. Question and answer are of speech, duality their sphere;
   Impossible in Monism to find them anywhere.
9. There is neither creation nor destruction, neither destiny nor free-will,
   Neither path nor achievement; this is the final truth.

APOLOGY TO HORNETS

One day when Bhagavan was climbing the Hill he knocked against a hornets' nest and was attacked and very badly stung in the leg and thigh. He felt remorse for having disturbed them. Asked why he felt remorse for what had happened accidentally, he replied:

    *   *   *   *   *

> When I was stung by hornets in revenge
> Upon the leg until it was inflamed,
> Although it was by chance I stepped upon
> Their nest, constructed in a leafy bush;
> What kind of mind is his if he does not
> At least repent for doing such a wrong?

SLEEP WHILE AWAKE

> Deep sleep can e'er be had while wide awake
> By search for Self. In dream and waking states
> Pursue the quest for Self without a break
> So long sleep's ignorance them permeates.

REPLY TO THE MOTHER

(DESTINY)

When Bhagavan left home his family tried to trace him but at first without success. Only some years later they discovered him at Tiruvannamalai. The Mother, not yet ripe to renounce the world and join him, went to try to persuade him to return to her. At this time he was not speaking, so he wrote the following verse for her, declaring that whatever is destined to happen will happen.

*   *   *   *   *

The fates of souls are all by God ordained
According to the deeds that they have done.
That end that's destined ne'er to be attained
Will never be achieved by anyone
However hard they try. All those things, too,
That it is destined must occur one day,
Will come to pass whatever you may do
To interfere and try their course to stay,
And this is certain. At length we come to see
That it is best that we should silent be.

FOR THE MOTHER'S RECOVERY

In 1914 Bhagavan's mother paid a brief visit to him at Tiruvanna-malai. While there she had a severe attack of fever, which some thought to be typhoid. Her life was despaired of and Bhagavan wrote the following poem for her recovery. Needless to say, she recovered. Two years later she came and took up her abode permanently at Bhagavan's ashram on the hill.

*   *   *   *   *

Oh Lord! Hill of my refuge, who curest the ills of recurrent births, it is for Thee to cure my mother's fever.

Oh God who slayest death! Reveal Thy feet in the Heart-Lotus of her who bore me to take refuge at Thy Lotus-Feet, and shield her from death. What is death if scrutinized?

Arunachala, Thou blazing fire of Knowledge! Enfold my mother in Thy Light and make her one with Thee. What need then for cremation?[1]

Arunachala, Dispeller of illusion! Why dost Thou delay to dispel my mother's delirium?[2] Is there any but Thee to watch as a Mother over one who has sought refuge in Thee and to rescue from the tyranny of karma?

---

[1] In India the body of the Sage is buried after death, whereas others are cremated. Having passed through the fire during life, he does not need to do so again after death. The Mother attained Liberation before death and was buried, as this verse foresees.

[2] By delirium is meant not merely the physical fever but the 'I-am-the-body' illusion.

FIVE VERSES ON THE SELF

Bhagavan wrote the following stanzas spontaneously, without being prompted or requested by any one. They were something of a *tour de force*, as he wrote them first in Telugu but to a Tamil metrical form and then himself translated them into Tamil.

* * * * *

1. He who is forgetful of the Self, mistaking the physical body for it, and goes through innumerable births, is like one who wanders all over the world in a dream. Thus realizing the Self would only be like waking up from the dream-wanderings.

2. One who asks himself 'Who am I?' and 'Where am I?', though existing all the while as the Self, is like a drunken man who enquires about his own identity and whereabouts.

3. While in fact the body is in the Self, he who thinks that the Self is within the insentient body is like one who considers the cloth of the screen which supports a cinema picture to be contained within the picture.

4. Does an ornament exist apart from the gold of which it is made? Where is the body apart from the Self? He who considers the body to be himself is an ignorant man. He who regards himself as the Self is the Enlightened One who has realized the Self.

5. The One Self, the Sole Reality, alone exists eternally. When even the Ancient Teacher, Dakshinamurti, revealed It through speechless eloquence, who else could convey it by speech?

RAMANA ARUNACHALA

In the recesses of the lotus-shaped hearts of all, beginning with Vishnu, there shines as pure intellect (Absolute Consciousness) the Paramatman who is the same as Arunachala or Ramana. When the mind melts with love of Him, and reaches the inmost recess of the Heart wherein He dwells as the Beloved, the subtle eye of pure intellect opens and He reveals Himself as Pure Consciousness.

THE SELF IN THE HEART

The eminent poet and sadhu, Ganapati Sastri, wrote in Sanskrit verse an account of certain questions that he and others put to Sri Bhagavan and of the answers they received. This was published by Sri Ramanasramam both in English and Sanskrit under the title *Sri Ramana Gita*. The following verse in it was composed by Bhagavan himself and translated by him into English as follows, although in general he did not write in English as his knowledge of the language was not great.

The verse enumerates three ways of realizing the Self: by Self-enquiry, which is the path of *jnana* or Knowledge; by turning inwards, which is the path of *bhakti* or devotion; and by breath-control, which is the path of Yoga. In this it is to be compared with the last of the Five Hymns to Arunachala.

*　　　*　　　*　　　*　　　*

> In the inmost core, the Heart
> Shines as Brahman alone,
> As 'I-I', the Self aware.
> Enter deep into the Heart
> By search for Self, or diving deep,
> Or with breath under check.
> Thus abide ever in Atman.
>
> (Ramana Gita, ch. 11, v. 2.)

PART TWO

Adaptations and Translations

7

The Song Celestial

BHAGAVAN was speaking once with a visiting pandit about the great merits of the Bhagavad Gita, when a devotee complained that it was difficult to keep all the 700 verses in mind and asked if there was not one verse that could be remembered as the quintessence of the Gita. Bhagavan thereupon mentioned Book X, verse 20: 'I am the Self, Oh Gudakesa, dwelling in the Heart of every being; I am the beginning and the middle and also the end of all beings.' Then he selected the 42 verses that here follow (of which that quoted above comes fourth) and arranged them in an appropriate order to serve as guidance.

* * * * *

Sanjaya said:

1. To him (Arjuna) thus filled with compassion and in despair, his eyes distressed and full of tears, spoke Madhusudana these words:

The Blessed Lord said:

2. This body, Oh son of Kunti, is called the *kshetra* (Field); Him who knows it, the Sages call, the *kshetrajna* (Knower of the Field).

3. Know Me also as the Knower of the Field in all the Fields, Oh Bharata: knowledge of the Field and of the Knower of the Field I deem to be true Knowledge.

4. I am the Self, Oh Gudakesa, dwelling in the Heart of every being; I am the beginning and the middle and also the end of all beings.

5. Of those born the death is certain, and certain the birth of

those dead: therefore for what none can prevent thou shouldst not grieve.

6. Never is He born nor does He die; nor, having been, ceaseth He any more to be: unborn, abiding, eternal, ancient, He is not slain when the body is slain.

7. Not to be cleft is He, not to be burnt is He, not even to be wetted nor yet to be dried is He: abiding He is and all-pervading, stable, immovable, and from everlasting.

8. Know That to be indestructible whereby all this is pervaded; of this Immutable none can work destruction.

9. Of the non-existent there is no being, and of what exists there is no not-being; the definite ascertainment of both is seen by the Seers of the Essence of Truth.

10. As ether everywhere present is not polluted by virtue of its subtlety, even so the Self abiding everywhere is not polluted in the body.

11. Nor sun nor moon nor fire illumines It: and whither having gone men return not, That is My Supreme Abode.

12. Unmanifested, Imperishable is this called; and this they proclaim the Supreme State, from which when once attained they return not, That is My Supreme Abode.

13. Without pride, without delusion, victorious over the blemish of attachment, ever abiding in the Self, their desires abandoned, released from the pairs called pleasure and pain, they go undeluded to that Immutable Abode.

14. He who forsakes the ordinances of the Scriptures, and acts under the influence of desire, attains not perfection, nor happiness, nor the Supreme State.

15. He who sees the Supreme Lord dwelling alike in all beings, perishing not as they perish, he it is who sees aright.

16. By devotion alone, without 'otherness', Oh Arjuna, can I be known and seen and in essence entered, Oh Parantapa.

17. The faith of every man, Oh Bharata, accords with his essential character; man is instinct with faith: as that wherein a man has faith, so is he.

18. He that has intense faith, and to that faith being devoted has the senses controlled, gains Knowledge; and having gained Knowledge he swiftly attains Supreme Peace.

19. To those who are self-attuned and who worship Me with loving devotion I give that union with understanding whereby they come to Me.

20. Out of compassion for them and abiding in their Self I destroy with the resplendent Light of Knowledge their darkness born of ignorance.

21. In those in whom ignorance is destroyed by Knowledge of the Self, Knowledge like the sun illumines That Supreme.

22. High, they say, are the senses; higher than the senses is the mind; and higher than the mind is the understanding; but one who is higher than understanding is He.

23. Thus knowing Him to be higher than the understanding, steadying the self by the Self, Oh thou strong of arm, slay the enemy in the form of desire, so hard to overcome.

24. Just as a burning fire makes ashes of its fuel, Oh Arjuna, even so does the Fire of Knowledge make ashes of all works.

25. Him whose every enterprise is without desire or motive, whose actions are burnt up in the Fire of Knowledge, the wise call a Sage.

26. All around the austere Sages, free from desire and wrath, who have subdued their mind and have realized the Self, radiates the beatific Peace of Brahman.

27. Little by little should one realize tranquillity, by judgment with a steadfast purpose; making the mind abide in the Self, one should think of nothing at all.

28. Towards whatsoever the mind wanders, being fickle and unsteady, therefrom it should be withdrawn and brought under the sway of the Self alone.

29. The saint who devoutly seeks Liberation, with the senses, mind, and intellect subdued, without desire, fear, or wrath, is indeed ever Liberated.

30. He who is steadfast in yoga and looks on everything impartially, sees the Self dwelling in all beings, and all beings in the Self.

31. I undertake to secure and protect the welfare of those who without 'otherness' meditate on Me and worship Me, and who ever abide thus attuned.

32. Of these the *Jnani*, who is ever attuned, whose devotion is

centred in One, is the most excellent; because to the *Jnani* I am exceedingly dear and he is dear to Me.

33. At the end of many births the *Jnani* finds refuge in Me, recognizing that Vasudeva is all. Such a high Soul is very hard to find.

34. When one puts away, Oh Partha, all the desires that are in the mind, and in the Self alone, by the Self, is well satisfied, then is one called a man of steadfast Wisdom.

35. That man attains Peace who, having cast away all desires, remains without longing, devoid of 'I' and 'mine'.

36. He by whom the world is not disturbed, and who is not disturbed by the world, free from exultation, impatience, fright, and agitation—he is dear to me.

37. He who holds honour and dishonour equal, equal the friendly party and the foe, who has renounced all enterprise—he is said to have transcended the *gunas*.

38. The man who revels here and now in the Self alone, with the Self is satisfied, and in the Self alone is content—for him there is no work to do.

39. For him there is no purpose either in doing work or in leaving it undone; nor is there in all beings anything which serves him as a purpose.

40. Content to take what chance may bring, having transcended the pairs of opposites, free from ill-will and even-minded in success or failure, though he works he is not bound.

41. The Lord, Oh Arjuna, dwells in the Heart of every being and His mysterious power spins round all beings set on the wheel.

42. To Him alone surrender, Oh Bharata, with all thy being; by His Grace shalt thou obtain Peace Supreme, the Abode Eternal.

8

Translations from the Agamas

THE Agamas are traditional Hindu scriptures regarded as no less authoritative and authentic than the Vedas. They are regarded as divinely revealed teachings and no human authorship is ascribed to them. Temple worship is mainly founded upon them.

There are twenty-eight Agamas that are accepted as authorities. From among them *Sarva Jnanottara* and *Devikalottara* are outstanding as expressing the standpoint of pure *Advaita* or nonduality. *Atma Sakshatkara* is the most essential part of *Sarva Jnanottara*.

The Maharshi spontaneously translated both these Agamas into Tamil verse, *Devikalottara* in the very early days when he was living in Virupaksha cave and *Atma-Sakshatkara* in 1933 when he was already in the Ashram at the foot of the hill. Both are instructions in the Path of Knowledge given by Lord Siva, the former to his son Guha (another name for Subramaniam) and the latter to his wife, Parvati.

Verses 70–72 in *Devikalottara*, forbidding the harming even of plant life, are not to be taken as applying to aspirants on the path. No extremes of discipline or behaviour are demanded of them. Indeed, as is generally indicated in these two Agamas, questions of discipline, ritual, and behaviour are far less important on this path than any other, since it is a path which works directly on the heart, awakening spiritual knowledge.

ATMA SAKSHATKARA

(ALL-COMPREHENSIVE KNOWLEDGE)

BENEDICTORY VERSE

(OF SRI BHAGAVAN)

Atma-Sakshatkara which was taught by Iswara, the Self (of all) to (his son) Guha is now propounded in Tamil by the same lord, the dweller within me, the Ancient and the Supreme.

*   *   *   *   *

TEXT

1 and 2. I will tell you, Oh Guha! another method by means of which even the unqualified, impalpable, subtle, and immanent Absolute can be clearly realized, by which realization the wise become themselves Siva. This has not hitherto been expounded to any other. Now listen!

3. It has been transmitted through a line of Gurus, but is still not explained by the different systems of philosophy. Its purpose is to rescue one from the bonds of *samsara*. It is transcendental and applicable to all.

4 and 5. 'I am He who is immanent in all, the soul of all, found everywhere, of the nature of the fundamentals, incomprehensible, ruling over all, beyond the fundamentals, beyond speech and mind, and without a name.' Such should be the worship, keeping the mind at the same time perfectly composed.

6 and 7. That which is unqualified, absolute Knowledge, eternal, steady, infinite, indescribable, being no effect of a precedent cause, without parallel and without form, undecaying, calm, transcending the senses, unmanifested, and yet ascertained without a doubt, is I myself.

8. I am certainly the Supreme God whose very being is all the *mantras* and who transcends them and extends beyond creation and destruction.

9. I permeate all this—visible and invisible, mobile and immobile, I am surely the Lord of all and from me all shine forth.

10. This Universe including the worlds and divided into several shapes, from *Shakti* down to the Earth, is all in me.

11. Whatever is seen or heard of in the Universe, both within and without, is permeated by me.

12. He who worships, thinking that he is a separate Self from Siva, the Supreme, does so out of ignorance and cannot himself become Siva.

13. Giving up the separate identity of yourself as distinct from Siva, meditate constantly on the non-dual unity: 'I am He who is known as Siva.'

14. One who is established in the contemplation of non-dual Unity will abide in the Self of everyone and realize the immanent, all-pervading One. There is no doubt of this.

15. He has perfect Wisdom who is a yogi firmly established in non-duality and free from thoughts.

16. The Self who is in the scriptures described as the unborn Lord, without form or qualities, is my Self. There is no doubt of this.

17. He who is not aware of the Self is an animal subject to creation, preservation and destruction, whereas he who is ever aware is Siva, eternal and pure. There is no doubt of this.

18. Carefully distinguishing the transcendental from the commonplace, the subtle from the gross, the Self must always be investigated into and realized by the vigilant.

19. The transcendental is the Highest and is also Nirvana, whereas the commonplace is subject to creation. *Mantras* represent the gross side whereas meditation represents the subtle side.

20 and 21. Oh Shadanana! (Six-Faced God) What is the use of putting it in so many words? Multiplicity of form exists only in the Self and the forms are externalized by the confused mind; they are objectively created simultaneously with thoughts of them.

22. Knowledge of the Self has thus been stated briefly to you, knowing which one realizes that everything is Atma only.

23. There is no place for gods, vedas, sacrifices, or gifts in this scheme. Become established in Realization of the Self which is pure and all-embracing.

24. For such as are submerged in the Ocean of destiny and desire protection there is no refuge anywhere except through Knowledge of the Self.

25. He who becomes established as the Self and realizes clearly is liberated without any effort on his part, even though he may be engaged in activity.

26. There is no gain higher than the Self. Realize that Self which is beyond the ego.

27. He is neither *prana* nor *aprana*, nor any organ or sense. Meditate on the Self who is eternal, perfect, and all-wise.

28. Concentrate the mind neither within, nor without, nor far, nor near, but on pure Transcendence.

29. Realize the Self always to be neither above nor below, nor on either side, not without nor within, but to be eternal and shining beyond the sublime void.

30. Realize the Self as pervading and subsisting in the void and in the non-void, as different from both void and non-void, not as intermediate between them, nor as partly void and partly non-void.

31. Realize the Self to be undefiled, unsupported, beyond caste, creed, name, or form, uncontaminated, and unqualified.

32. Realize the Self to be without abode, unsupported, immeasurable, unparalleled, inherently pure, and eternal.

33. Renouncing all activities, desireless and not associated in any manner, abiding in the Self, one should meditate on the Self with the Self and in the Self.

34. Let the wise man meditate on the Self after divesting himself of the ideas of place, caste, creed, and duties pertaining thereto.

35. This is the *mantra* to repeat; this is the *devata* to worship; this is meditation; this is penance; *to eradicate all thoughts and seek the Self.*

36. Making the meditation abstract and without physical support and fixing the mind on the Self, remain unagitated by thoughts.

37. It is not something that can be thought of, nor anything that cannot be thought of; it is both thought and non-thought. Realize the Self which is not attached in any manner.

38 and 39. Not allowing the mind to cling to anything, engage always in what transcends thought. Such happiness as is found in the state of void and of purity is also inherent in the Self, undistracted, unimaginable, not the result of any antecedent cause; it is also unparalleled. It is said to be the best, the highest, and peerless.

40. Undistracted by the senses, liberate the mind from its functions. When it transcends itself, the highest bliss results.

41. Yoga is to be unceasingly practised wherever one may be. There is no difference in Jnana whatever be the caste or status of the person.

42. Just as milk is uniformly white though drawn from cows of different colours, so also Realization is uniform for all persons of whatever denominations.

43. Brahman is everywhere, immanent in all, and all-pervading. There are no qualifications. Hence do not heed the particulars but concentrate on absolute Brahman.

44. There is nothing for him to accomplish; therefore he reaps no fruits of his actions, nor is he obliged to be active; there is no distinctive caste, creed, or code of conduct for one inhering·in the Supreme Self.

45 and 46. However engaged and in whatever environment he may be, he who is established in the Self is always in repose; and he who is content with the Self is always pure.

47. 'Though moving, I do not come nor go, for there is no motion for me. I was not born nor shall ever be reborn; for I am not concerned with what pertains to the body.

48. 'Actions are of the body, and the body is the result of actions. I do not act in any way nor am I associated with the body;' thus thinks the perfect, regenerated one.

49. 'Further the body is no bondage for me, for I am ever-free; the physical accompaniments can never affect the Self.'

50. Just as light shines, dispelling darkness, so also the Supreme Self shines, dispelling ignorance.

51. Just as a lamp spontaneously goes out if not fed with oil, so also the ego becomes extinct if one meditates unceasingly and becomes merged in the Self. There is no higher gain than the Self.

52. When a pot is moved from place to place the space inside it appears to move too but the movement pertains to the pot and

not to the space within. So it is with the soul which corresponds to the space in the pot.

53. When the pot is broken its inner space merges in the outer expanse; similarly with the death of the gross body the Spirit merges in the Absolute.

54. Thus has the truth been expounded authoritatively by the omniscient and competent Master. So liberate yourself from bondage and be metamorphosed into the Omniscient and Infinite.

55. Turn away from all scriptures; engage in the pure *yoga* of Self-realization; being convinced that nothing excels this Supreme Knowledge, hold the mind from straying.

56. Engaged in this way the wise man merges for ever in the impalpable Reality; he becomes all-pervading, attains Liberation, abides immanent in all—within and without—and wanders at will.

57. Becoming ethereal and pure, he merges in Siva—synonymous with Omniscience, contentment, eternal consciousness, independence, and eternal, undecaying, and infinite power.

58 and 59. No regulations are binding on him such as incantations, worship, ablutions, sacrificial fire, or other disciplinary actions; he does not reap the fruit of actions—virtuous or otherwise; there is no ancestor-worship for him; he need observe no fasts on specified days or occasions, nor need he worry about renunciation, household, or celibacy and their obligations.

60. Drink of the nectar of Siva-Knowledge and conduct yourself as you please. You are the same as Siva in immortality and purity, but not in the power to create, etc.

61. All this is the Truth and nothing but the Truth. Oh Guha! This is the final Truth. There is nothing else to be known.

62. He who is pure of mind, intellect, and ego, the senses and their perceptions, is pure in fact and finds everything pure as well.

63. Give up walking through fire and bathing in the Ganges and other rivers and in waterfalls; drink of the nectar of Supreme Siva-Knowledge. Become in the form of the Lord eternally and in all purity. Have done with creating and roam about at your ease.

DEVIKALOTTARA

INTRODUCTION BY SRI MAHARSHI

Sri Devikalottara is one of the minor Agamas, and this chapter from it on *Jnana-achara-vichara* is what the Supreme Siva vouchsafed to His beloved—a discourse on the wisdom into which ripe souls in their maturity are initiated and their mode of life. Thus, this work, being the essence of all the Agamas, is a wonderful boat that lifts up and carries to the shore of freedom those souls who are struggling hard for their lives, sinking down and rising in the sea of *samsara* with its rotation of births and deaths. May all aspirants, with its help, desist from their confused rambling, take the direct path pointed out therein and reach that supreme Abode of quiet Bliss.

* * * * *

1. Devi: Oh Lord of the Celestials! Be so gracious as to instruct me in the means of Liberation, in *Jnana* and in the conduct of *Jnanis*, hearing which Liberation may result to all.

2. Isvara.[1] Oh Fair One! I shall forthwith describe to you the conduct of *Jnanis*, on account of which they are absolved from all sins and delivered from *samsara*.

3. Even millions of books cannot impart right knowledge to such as are unable to find it in *Kala Jnana* (this Agama).

4. Therefore, let the wise man be fearless, undoubting, free from desire, earnest, resolute, and persevering in *Jnana*, as explained here.

5. Let the aspirant for Liberation behave in an unselfish and kind way and give aid to all, let him undergo penance, and let him study this Agama.

6. He is Brahma, he is Deva, he is Vishnu, he is Indra, he is

---

[1] The name 'Isvara' means 'God' and can therefore be used, as here, in place of 'Siva'.

the six-faced Skanda, he is the master of all Devas (Brishaspati), he is the Yogi, and he alone is rich in *tapas*.

7. He alone is learned, he alone fortunate and successful, whose mind is no longer unstable as air but is held firm.

8. That is the way to Liberation, that is the highest virtue, that is wisdom, that is strength, and that is the merit of those who seek.

9. The stabilization of the restless mind is the only true pilgrimage, the only alms-giving and the only penance.

10. The mind when outgoing is *samsara*; when steady it is *Moksha* (Liberation). Therefore let the mind be held firm by supreme Wisdom.

11. Where there is pure unbroken happiness (in solitude), there is Infinity. Is there a wise man who will not revel in the unshaken, absolute Reality?

12. One who has recoiled from sensual pleasures and devoted himself to undefiled, pure wisdom, is sure to achieve everlasting *Moksha*, even if he does not consciously seek it.

13. The mere consciousness of being as Awareness is itself *Shakti* and all this world is the projection of this *Shakti*. The true State of Knowledge is that in which the mind is not attached to this *Shakti*.

14. Recognition of the world as the manifestation of *Shakti* is worship of *Shakti*. Pure Knowledge, unrelated to objects, is absolute.

15. Do not waste time meditating on *chakras*, *nadis*, *padmas*, or *mantras* of deities, or their forms.

16. If you desire eternal *Moksha* do not engage in Yogic practices or incantations, or anything else of the kind.

17. There is no worship, or prayer, or incantation, or meditation. There is nothing to be known apart from the Self.

18. Outgoing minds forge chains of bondage for themselves. Checking the outgoing mind frees one from misery in the world.

19. There is nothing within or without, up or down, midway or sideways. What is perfect is of all forms, yet without any definite form for itself—and shines in its own Awareness.

20. Since whatever a person sees, thinks of, and seeks to accomplish by his actions influences his destiny, let him meditate on that which is beyond perception, and even imagination.

21. There is in truth no cause, no result, and no action; all that is chimerical. There is no world and no dweller in it.

22. The Universe has no external support, nor is it cognized from without; but as you make it so it becomes.

23. He who meditates not on the etheral, all-pervading Void, gets entangled in *samsara* like the silkworm in its self-made cocoon.

24. Howsoever born, in whatever genus, there is endless misery for the individual over and over again, in every birth; in order to avert this one should meditate on the infinite Void.

25. The path has been prescribed only with a view to acquire Knowledge. Turn away from any kind of Yoga involving action, and meditate on the Void.

26. Only those heroes who, with the arrow of the Void, have pierced through all regions from the highest to the nethermost, are considered Knowers of this Void.

27. By fixing the wandering mind (more mischievous even than a monkey) in the all-empty Void, one reaches Nirvana.

28 and 29. May he enjoy bliss who realizes the Supreme, beatific, formless One, who is all-pervading as ether, manifested as *tattvas* (fundamentals) themselves, but separate from the body, not alloyed with perceptions like 'I am', but pure all-covering awareness.

30. Just as fire is automatically extinguished if not fed with fuel, so does the mind become extinct if not fed with thoughts.

31. Turn away from confusion, ignorance, delusion, dream, sleep, or wakefulness; for the Supreme is different from the gross body, from the subtle *prana*, from thought or intellect or ego; meditate on *Chit* (Consciousness) and become one with it.

33. The mind often strays into reverie or falls asleep; be vigilant and turn it to its pristine state again and again.

34. When once it becomes steady the mind should be left undisturbed; nothing should be thought of, only the mind should be stabilized in its original state.

35. The mind seeks attachment and this causes it to wander. Destroy its attachments so as to turn it inward and stabilize it there. Do not disturb it when there.

36. Just as space is unaffected by contact with the elements, similarly one's Primal State is unaffected by contact with objects. Meditate on that.

37. Only then is life's purpose fulfilled. Pure Knowledge alone is capable of holding the fickle mind steady.

38. The mind should not dwell on what is above, below, midway, or within; it should always remain unattached.

39. If asleep awaken the mind; if distracted calm it; if neither asleep nor distracted do not disturb it.

40. When the mind is thus left without anything to cling to and does not clutch at anything and is quite free from thoughts it indicates *Mukti*.

41. Rescue the mind from qualities, make it pure and fix it in the Heart. That consciousness which manifests clearly thereafter must alone be aimed at and striven for.

42. Those who meditate on the absolute Void and practise to that end become established in that ineffable state which is beyond birth and death.

43. Gods and goddesses, merits, demerits, and their fruits, knowledge of the support and of the supported are all signs of bondage in *samsara*.

44. Qualities are the pairs of opposites; turn away from them and the highest realization results. Such a yogi is the *Jivanmukta*; on discarding the body he becomes *Videhamukta*.

45. Never should the body be given up in disgust by a wise man; it dies of itself as soon as *prarabdha karma* is exhausted.

46. There is in the Heart the infinite Consciousness 'I–I', which is at the same time pure and constant; on eradicating the ego this manifests and leads to *Moksha*.

47. Such 'I–I' is 'That' which is beyond qualifications and eternal as Consciousness. Contemplating without break that 'I–I' as Siva, shake off attachments.

48. Break away from all relationship of country, status, caste, and its duties and think always of your own natural state.

49. I am alone and nothing is mine, nor do I pertain to anything else; I can find none whose I am or who is mine.

50. I am the Supreme Brahman! I am the Lord of the Universe! Such is the settled conviction of the *Mukta*; all other experiences lead to bondage.

51. When the Self is clearly realized not to be the body the realizer gains peace and becomes free from all desires.

52. He who in the scriptures is described as the unborn, ever-existent Lord of all is the same as the disembodied, unqualified Self in each; I am He without a doubt.

53. I am Awareness pure and simple; I am ever free; I am indeterminable, neither grasped nor lost but indescribable. I am therefore Brahman and ever blissful.

54 and 55. I am what is covered from head to foot, within and without, as far as the enveloping skin and separate also, being immortal, the living, conscious, ever-present Self. I am the Lord of all, the motionless and the moving. I am the father, the mother, and the grandparents. It is ME that the aspirants for *Mukti* contemplate being established in the fourth state (i.e. the *Turiya* state—the substratum beneath the waking, dream, and sleep states).

56. I alone am worthy of worship among the gods and men, the serpents, celestial beings, sacrifices, etc., and all worship ME alone.

57. All worship ME alone through purificatory penance, or by giving of various gifts. All creation is in ME and I am their Being.

58. I am not gross, nor subtle, nor void; I am live Consciousness and the sole Refuge of the universe. I am the eternal pure Lord of all, not bounded by the dream and other states, but transcending all creation.

59 and 60. Discern at every step that I am whatever is beginningless, conscious, unborn, primal, resident in the Heart-cavity, unsullied, and transcending the world, whatever is pure, peerless, desireless, beyond sight or other perceptions or even mental apprehension. Whatever is eternal is Brahman. He who is unshaken in such certitude is sure to change into Brahman and be immortal.

61. Fair One! Knowledge has thus been expounded here for gaining Liberation. Listen now to the conduct of the Enlightened.

62. He requires no ablutions, nor prayer, nor worship, nor *homa* (fire-worship), nor other discipline; he need not worship fire or engage in any such activity.

63. He is not bound by disciplinary codes, nor need he frequent temples for worship; he need not perform *sraddha* or go on pilgrimages or observe vows.

64. He does not reap the fruit of actions, whether religious rites or worldly activities; on the contrary he is absolved once and for all from every kind of action and code of conduct.

65. Let the aspirant give up conventional usages and traditional practices, as being chains of bondage for him.

66. Let him not accept thaumaturgic powers or amulets even when directly offered to him.

67. For all these are like ropes to tether a beast, and they will certainly drag him downward. Supreme Liberation does not lie that way; it is not found elsewhere than in Infinite Consciousness.

68. One must engage in Yoga by every means in one's power, however else one may be engaged. Festivities should be avoided even if they are in temples, *mutts*, or other such sacred places.

69. Spiritual advancement does not admit of even the slightest harm to a worm, reptile, insect, tree, or life in any form.

70. Therefore let no vegetable life be destroyed, nor even leaves injured. No pain should be caused to any created being or thing. Even flowers should not be plucked.

71 and 72. Even worship should be performed with flowers that have fallen from the trees of themselves. One should not interest oneself in mischievous or harmful prayers, such as *marana* etc., (causing death or pain to enemies or obtaining favours from the great or love from the beloved). Worship of images should not form an end in itself.

73. Giving up all interest in the worship of sacred places and images and in the performance of religious rites pertaining thereto, engage yourself in meditating on universal *Chit* (Consciousness).

74. Dispassion is equanimity in pleasure and pain, among friends and foes, with pebble or with gold.

75. A Yogi should not be swayed by desires nor yield to gratifying the senses. He should find ecstasy in the Self alone, free from desire and fear.

76. Equanimity must always be maintained, whether praised or slandered; equal conduct must be observed towards all creatures and there should be no discrimination between the Self and Non-Self.

77. Disputes, worldly associations and quarrels should be avoided. Not even spiritual disputations should be indulged in, whether good or bad.

78. Jealousy, slander, pomp, passion, envy, love, anger, fear and misery should all disappear gradually and entirely.

79. If a man is free from the pairs of opposites and lives in solitude, perfect wisdom shines in him even in the present body.

80. As Liberation results from Knowledge, thaumaturgic powers are useless; only the aspirant who still craves worldly enjoyments desires these powers.

81. If only the soul knows its true Master, Liberation is certain, whether attended by Supernatural powers or not.

82. The body is composed of five elements and Siva dwells therein; from Siva down to the Earth all are manifestations of Sankara.[1]

83 and 84. Earnest seekers who worship Enlightened Ones at sight, with perfume, flowers, water, fruits, incense, clothing, and food, or by word, deed, and thought, are absolved then and there. By praising them, they share their merits, by slandering them their demerits.

85. I have expounded the whole of the Path of Knowledge and the conduct pertaining thereto, as you desired. What more do you wish to know?

[1] A name of Siva.

9

Poems from Shankaracharya

I N THE eighth century A.D. pure Vedantic teaching, the doctrine of Advaita or Non-duality, which is the very essence of Hinduism, had shrunk to a low ebb and was restored to full vigour by the great spiritual Master Sri Shankara, known also as Shankaracharya or 'Shankara the Teacher'. Ramana Maharshi, being a perfect *Jnani*, that is one who is Liberated from illusion and established in Absolute Knowledge, accepted Sri Shankara's teaching as his own. From time to time he translated one or another of his works, either spontaneously or on the request of some devotee who did not read Sanskrit and required a Tamil version.

*   *   *   *   *

GURU STUTI

There is a story that Sri Shankara once challenged an opponent to a dispute, the understanding being that if he won his opponent was to renounce his family and go forth in the homeless state, but if his opponent won Shankara was to accept the life of a householder. The opponent was beaten on all points but then his wife intervened, claiming that she also should be heard as she and her husband were one and the penalty he would undergo if he lost affected her also. Sri Shankara granted this and she thereupon challenged him to expound the spiritual symbolism of sex. Never having experienced carnal love, he was at a loss and asked for two weeks' grace before answering, and this she granted.

At this time a king died and Sri Shankara, by his yogic power, left his own body and entered that of the dead king, so that it seemed to the latter's courtiers that he had miraculously recovered. The queens were overjoyed but, contrasting the intelligence, vigour, and grace that their husband now showed with the dull, inert fellow he had been formerly, they guessed what had happened. They therefore sent out officers with instructions to seek for the apparently dead body of a sadhu and to cremate any such that they found, so that the new king could not return to his former body. They did indeed come upon the apparently lifeless body of Sri Shankara and took it for cremation.

Sri Shankara, however, had taken the precaution of warning his disciples and had told them if he overstayed his time or if there was any danger to his body to go to his palace and sing the following song about the Truth. They did so and he immediately abandoned the king's body and revived his own. Sri Shankara thereafter met the wife of his opponent and, having now gained experience, accepted and won the contest.

The Maharshi translated this song under the title 'Guru-Stuti'.

*   *   *   *   *

1. That is the Truth which the wise realize as the Self, the residuum left over on withdrawing from external objects, with or without form (ether, air, fire, water, and earth), by a careful application of the scriptural text 'Not this—Not this'. That thou art!

2. That is the Truth which, after generating the fundamentals, (ether, air, fire, water, and earth) and entering the world, lies hidden beneath the five sheaths, and which has been threshed out by the wise with the pestle of discernment, just as the grain is recovered by threshing and winnowing the chaff. That thou art!

3. Just as wild horses are broken in by whipping and stabling them, so also the unruly senses, straying among objects, are lashed by the whip of discrimination, showing that objects are unreal, and are tethered by the rope of pure intellect to the Self by the wise. Such Self is the Truth. That thou art!

4. The Truth has been ascertained by the wise to be the substratum which is different from the waking, dream, and deep sleep states, its own expanded modes, which indeed are held

together by it like the flowers strung together on a garland. That thou art!

5. That is the Truth which the scriptures show to be the primal cause of all, elucidating the point clearly by such texts as 'Purusha is all this', 'like gold in ornaments of gold', etc. That thou art!

6. The Truth has been forcefully proclaimed by the scriptures in such texts as 'He who is in the Sun, is in man', 'He who shines in the Sun, shines in the right eye', etc. That thou art!

7. What pure Brahmins seek so eagerly by repetition of the Vedas, by religious gifts, by earnest application of their hard-earned knowledge, and by renunciation, is the Truth. That thou art!

8. That is the Truth which the valiant have got by seeking, with controlled mind, with abstinence, penance, etc., and by diving into the Self by the self. Realizing it they are considered to be heroes with their highest purpose accomplished. That is the transcendental Satchitananda (Being-Consciousness-Bliss) after gaining which there is nothing more to worry about since perfect peace reigns. That thou art!

SHANKARACHARYA'S HYMN TO DAKSHINAMURTI

(Translated from Bhagavan Ramana Maharshi's Tamil rendering)

According to Hindu legends, Dakshinamurti (which means 'South-ward-facing') is God or Siva manifested as a youth who is the Divine Guru and guides disciples older than himself through silent influence on their Heart. The name is also divided as Dakshina-amurti and taken to mean 'Formless Power'.

The Maharshi was Siva manifested, the Divine Guru who taught through Silence and was therefore identified with Dakshina-murti.

*　　　*　　　*　　　*　　　*

INVOCATION

That Shankara who appeared as Dakshinamurti to grant peace to the Great Ascetics (Sanaka, Sanandana, Sanat Kumara and Sanat Sujata), who revealed his real state of silence, and who has expressed the nature of the Self in this Hymn, abides in me.

*　　　*　　　*　　　*　　　*

THE HYMN

He who teaches through silence the nature of the supreme Brahman, who is a youth, who is the most eminent Guru surrounded by the most competent disciples that remain steadfast in Brahman, who has the hand-pose indicating illumination,[1] who is of the nature of bliss,

---

[1] There are many traditional *mudras* or postures of the hands which are used in Indian dancing and iconography, each of which has its own meaning.

who revels in himself, who has a benign countenance—that Father who has a south-facing form,[2] we adore.

To him who by Maya, as by dream, sees within himself the universe which is inside him, like a city that appears in a mirror, (but) which is manifested as if externally to him who apprehends, at the time of awakening, his own single Self, to him, the primal Guru, Dakshinamurti, may this obeisance be!

To him who like a magician or even like a great yogi displays, by his own power, this universe which at the beginning is undifferentiated like the sprout in the seed, but which is made differentiated under the varied conditions of space, time, and karma and posited by Maya: to him, the Guru Dakshinamurti, may this obeisance be!

To him whose luminosity alone, which is of the nature of existence, shines forth, entering the objective world which is like the nonexistent: to him who instructs those who resort to him through the text 'That thou art': to him by realizing whom there will be no more fall into the ocean of birth: to him who is the refuge of the ascetics, the Guru Dakshinamurti, may this obeisance be!

To him who is luminous like the light of a lamp set in a pot with many holes: to him whose knowledge moves outward through the eye and other sense organs: to him who is effulgent as 'I know', and the entire universe shines after him: to him, the unmoving Guru Dakshinamurti, may this obeisance be!

They who know the 'I' as body, breath, senses, intellect, or the Void, are deluded like women and children, and the blind and the stupid, and talk much. To him who destroys the great delusion produced by ignorance: to him who removes the obstacles to knowledge, the Guru Dakshinamurti, may this obeisance be!

To him who sleeps when the manifested mind gets resolved, on account of the veiling by Maya, like the sun or the moon in eclipse, and on waking recognizes self-existence in the form 'I have slept till now': to him the Guru of all that moves and moves not, Dakshinamurti, may this obeisance be!

To him who, by means of the hand-pose indicating illumination, manifests to his devotees his own Self that for ever shines within as

---

[2] The supreme Guru is the spiritual north pole and therefore traditionally faces southwards.

'I', constantly, in all the inconstant states such as infancy, etc., and waking, etc.—to him whose eye is of the form of the fire of knowledge, the Guru Dakshinamurti, may this obeisance be!

To the self who, deluded by Maya, sees, in dreaming and waking, the universe in its distinctions such as cause and effect, master and servant, disciple and teacher, and father and son, to him, the Guru of the world, Dakshinamurti, may this obeisance be!

To him whose eightfold form is all this moving and unmoving universe, appearing as earth, water, fire, air, ether, the sun, the moon, and soul: beyond whom, supreme and all-pervading, there exists naught else for those who enquire—to him the gracious Guru Dakshinamurti, may this obeisance be!

Since, in this Hymn, the all-self-hood has thus been explained, by listening to it, by reflecting on its meaning, by meditating on it, and by reciting it, there will come about lordship together with the supreme splendour consisting in all-self-hood; thence will be achieved, again, the unimpeded supernormal power presenting itself in eight forms.

10

Vivekachudamani

THIS work by Shankaracharya, together with the *Drik Drisya Viveka*, was translated into Tamil prose by Bhagavan while he was still living in Virupaksha Cave. It is a very free translation, even the order of the paragraphs being changed to some extent.

*   *   *   *   *

INTRODUCTION

by

BHAGAVAN SRI RAMANA MAHARSHI

Every being in the world yearns to be always happy and free from the taint of sorrow, and desires to get rid of bodily ailments, which are not of his true nature. Further, everyone cherishes the greatest love for himself, and this love is not possible in the absence of happiness. In deep sleep, though devoid of everything, one has the experience of being happy. Yet, due to the ignorance of the real nature of one's own being, which is happiness itself, people flounder in the vast ocean of material existence, forsaking the right path that leads to happiness, and act under the mistaken belief that the way to be happy consists in obtaining the pleasures of this and the other world.

Unfortunately, however, there is no such happiness which has not the taint of sorrow. It is precisely for the purpose of pointing out the straight path to true happiness that Lord Siva,

taking on the guise of Sri Shankaracharya, wrote the commentaries on the Triple Canon (*Prasthana Traya*) of the Vedanta,
which extol the excellence of this bliss; and that he demonstrated
it by his own example in life. These commentaries, however,
are of little use to those ardent seekers who are intent upon
realizing the bliss of Liberation but have not the scholarship
necessary for studying them.

It is for such as these that Sri Shankara revealed the essence
of the commentaries in this short treatise: 'The Crown-gem of
Discrimination', explaining in detail the points that have to be
grasped by those who seek Liberation, and thereby directing
them to the true and direct path.

Sri Shankara begins by observing that it is hard indeed to
attain human birth, and that, having attained it, one should
strive to achieve the bliss of Liberation, which is really only the
nature of one's being. By *Jnana* or Spiritual Knowledge alone is
this Bliss to be realized, and *Jnana* is achieved only through
vichara or steady enquiry. In order to learn this method of
enquiry, says Sri Shankara, one should seek the grace of a
Guru; and he then proceeds to describe the qualities of the Guru
and his disciple and how the latter should approach and serve
his master. He further emphasizes that in order to realize the
bliss of Liberation one's own individual effort is an essential
factor. Mere book-learning never yields this bliss, which can be
realized only through Self-enquiry or *vichara*, which consists of
sravana or devoted attention to the precepts of the Guru,
manana or deep contemplation and *nididhyasana* or the culti-
vation of equanimity in the Self.

The three bodies, physical, subtle, and causal, are non-self
and are unreal. The Self, that is the *Aham* or 'I', is quite different
from them. It is due to ignorance that the sense of Self or the 'I'
notion is foisted on that which is not Self, and this indeed is
bondage. Since from ignorance arises bondage, from Knowledge
ensues liberation. To know this from the Guru is *sravana*.

The process of *manana*, which is subtle enquiry or deep
contemplation, consists in rejecting the three bodies consisting
of the five sheaths, (physical, vital, mental, intellectual, and
blissful) as not 'I' and discovering through subtle enquiry of

'Who am I?' that which is different from all three and exists single and universal in the heart as *Aham* or 'I', just as a stalk of grass is delicately drawn out from its sheath. This 'I' is denoted by the word *tvam* (in the Scriptural dictum, '*Tat-tvam-asi*' That thou art).

The world of name and form is but an adjunct of *Tat* or Brahman and, having no separate reality, is rejected as reality and affirmed as nothing else but Brahman. The instruction of the disciple by the Guru in the *Mahavakya Tat-tvam-asi*, which declares the identity of the Self and the Supreme, is his *upadesa.* (spiritual guidance). The disciple is then enjoined to remain in the beatific state of Aham-Brahman (I-the Absolute). Nevertheless, the old tendencies of the mind sprout up thick and strong and constitute an obstruction. These tendencies are threefold and ego is their root. The ego flourishes in the externalized and differentiating consciousness caused by the forces of projection due to *rajas* and veiling due to *tamas*.

To fix the mind firmly in the heart until these forces are destroyed and to awaken with unswerving, ceaseless vigilance the true and cognate tendency which is characteristic of the Atman and is expressed by the sayings: *Aham Brahmasmi* (I am Brahman), and Brahmaivaham (Brahman alone am I), is termed *nididhyasana* or *Atmanusandhana*, that is constancy in the Self. This is otherwise called *bhakti*, yoga, and *dhyana*.

Atmanusandhana has been compared to churning curds in order to make butter, the mind being compared to the churn, the heart to the curds, and the practice of concentration on the Self to the process of churning. Just as butter is made by churning the curds and fire by friction, so the natural and changeless state of *nirvikalpa samadhi* is produced by unswerving vigilant concentration on the Self, ceaseless like the unbroken flow of oil. This readily and spontaneously yields that direct, immediate, unobstructed, and universal perception of Brahman, which is at once knowledge and experience and which transcends time and space.

This perception is Self-realization. Achieving it cuts the knot of the heart. The false delusions of ignorance, the vicious and age-long tendencies of the mind which constitute this knot are destroyed. All doubts are dispelled and the bondage of karma is severed.

Thus in this Crown-Gem of Discrimination has Sri Shankara described *samadhi* or spiritual trance which is the limitless Bliss of Liberation, beyond doubt and duality, and at the same time has indicated the means for its attainment. To attain this state of freedom from duality is the real purpose of life, and only he who has done so is a *Jivanmukta*, liberated while yet alive, not one who has a mere theoretical understanding of what constitutes *purushartha* or the desired end and aim of human endeavour.

Thus defining a *Jivanmukta*, Sri Shankara declares him to be free from the bonds of threefold karma (*sanchita, agami,* and *prarabdha*). The disciple attains this state and then relates his personal experience. He who is liberated is indeed free to act as he pleases, and when he leaves the body, he abides in Liberation and never returns to this birth which is death.

Sri Shankara thus describes Realization, that is Liberation, as twofold, *Jivanmukti* and *Videhamukti*, as explained above. Moreover, in this short treatise, written in the form of a dialogue between a Guru and his disciple, he has considered many other relevant topics.

(By Courtesy of the *Sunday Times*, Madras.)

*   *   *   *   *

INVOCATION

Rejoice eternally! The heart rejoices at the feet of the Lord, who is the Self, shining within as 'I–I' eternally, so that there is no (alternation of) night and day. This will result in removal of ignorance of Self.

*   *   *   *   *

PRAISE TO THE GURU

Sri Shankara Jagathguru shines as the form of Lord Siva. In this work, *Vivekachudamani*, he has expounded in detail the heart of

Vedanta and its meaning in order that the most ardent of those qualified for Liberation may acquaint themselves with it and attain immortality.

Homage to the ever blissful Sri Govinda Sadguru who is to be known only by the ultimate truth of Vedanta and not by any other standard.

*　　　*　　　*　　　*　　　*

THE TEXT

It is indeed very difficult to obtain a human body. Even though one does, it is very difficult to become a Brahmin. Even if one becomes one, it is still more difficult to walk in the path of Vaidik Dharma in which the Vedas are chanted. Still more difficult is it to become a perfect scholar, and more difficult again to undertake enquiry into the Self and the non-Self. Yet more difficult than all this is it to obtain wisdom born of experience of the Self. Liberation in the form of abidance as the Self, born of that wisdom, is not to be attained except as a result of righteous actions performed throughout countless crores of births. However, even though all the above qualifications may not be obtained, Liberation is assured through the Grace of the Lord if only three conditions are obtained: that is a human birth, intense desire for Liberation, and association with Sages.

If, by some great penance, that rarity a human body is obtained, with its ability to understand the meaning of the scriptures, and yet, owing to attachment to insentient things, effort is not made to attain the immutable state of Liberation, which is one's own true state, then indeed one is a fool committing suicide. What greater fool is there than one who does not seek his own good?

Liberation is not to be achieved through endless cycles of time by reading the scriptures or worshipping the gods or by anything else than knowledge of the unity of Brahman and Atman. Wealth or actions made possible by wealth cannot produce the yearning for Liberation. Therefore the scriptures have rightly declared that action can never produce Liberation. In order to obtain Liberation one must heroically renounce even the very desire for the pleasures of this world. Then one must seek the Perfect Guru who is the embodiment of Peace and must concentrate one's mind and meditate ceaselessly on that into which one is initiated. Such meditation leads to abidance in the wisdom of the experience obtained. Embarking in that ship of wisdom, one must ferry over to the shore of Liberation that Self which is immersed in the ocean of *samsara*. Therefore the courageous aspirant should give up attachment to wife, sons, and property and give up all activity. By so doing he should free himself from bondage to the cycle of birth and death and seek Liberation. Actions are prescribed only for purification of the mind, not for realization of the Self. Knowledge of the truth of the Self is obtained only by Self-enquiry and not by any number of actions. One who mistakes a rope for a serpent is cast into fear thereby and his fear and distress can be removed only by the knowledge that it is a rope. A friend who knows this tells him so and he investigates and finds that it is so. There is no other way. Similarly, knowledge of Brahman is obtained through initiation by the Guru and enquiry into Truth. That Truth cannot be realized through purificatory baths, offerings, breath-control, or any other practice. He who seeks Liberation through knowledge of the Self must enquire into the Self with the help of the perfect Guru who, being free from desires, is a knower of Brahman and an Ocean of Grace. It is mainly through enquiry that he who is competent achieves knowledge of the Self; circumstance, time, and the Grace of the Lord are but aids to the quest.

In order to be qualified for enquiry into the Self, a man must have a powerful intellect and ability to seize the essential and reject the inessential besides the various qualities enumerated in the scriptures. What are these? He must be able to discriminate between the Real and the unreal. He must have an unattached mind. He must possess control over the outer and inner sense organs. He must ardently desire Liberation. And he must be tireless in practice. Only such a one is qualified to enquire into the Brahman. The qualifications are enumerated as follows:

1. Discrimination between the Real and the unreal.
2. Disinclination to enjoy the fruits of one's actions either in this or in any future life.

3. The six virtues of tranquillity, self-control, withdrawal, forbearance, faith, and concentration of the Self.

4. Intense yearning for Liberation.

The aspirant must indeed have these qualities in order to attain abidance in the Self; without them there can be no realization of the Truth. Let us see what these are:

1. Discrimination between the Real and the unreal is the firm conviction that Brahman alone is the Truth and that the world is unreal.

2. We both observe and learn from the scriptures that all pleasures experienced by animate beings, from Brahma downwards, are transient and impermanent and involve sorrows and imperfections; giving up the desire for them is *vairagya* or non-attachment.

3(*a*) Tranquillity implies fixing the mind upon its target by meditating frequently on the imperfections of things and becoming dissatisfied with them.

(*b*) Self-control means controlling the outer and inner sense organs and fixing them in their respective centres.

(*c*) Withdrawal means giving up all outer activity by fixing the mind on its target so firmly that it is not led by its previous tendencies to dwell on objects.

(*d*) Forbearance means the endurance of any sorrows that may befall without trying to avoid them.

(*e*) Faith, which is the cause of Self-realization, is the outcome of firm conviction of the truth of Vedantic scriptures and of the words of the Guru.

(*f*) Concentration is making every effort to fix the mind on the pure Brahman despite its wandering nature.

These are said to be the six qualifications needed for the practice of *samadhi*.

4. Intense yearning for Liberation arises from the desire to free oneself by realizing one's true nature, attaining freedom from the bondage of the body and ego which is caused by ignorance. This yearning may be of different grades. It may be only dull or medium, but it may be highly developed by means of the six qualifications mentioned above, and in this case it can bear fruit. If the yearning is intense these qualifications speedily bear fruit. But if renunciation

and yearning are weak the result may be a mere appearance like a mirage in the desert.

Of all the means leading to Liberation, *bhakti* or devotion is the best; and this *bhakti* means seeking the truth of one's own Self, so say the Sages.

The aspirant who possesses the necessary qualifications and wishes to undertake Self-enquiry must seek a Sad-Guru and bow down to him with humility, awe, and reverence and serve him in various ways. The Sad-Guru is one capable of destroying the bondage of those who adhere to him. He is an ocean of immutable wisdom. His knowledge is all-comprehensive. He is pure as crystal. He has attained victory over desires. He is supreme among the knowers of Brahman. He rests calmly in Brahman like a fire that has consumed its fuel. He is an endless reservoir of mercy. There is no explanation why he is merciful; it is his very nature. He befriends all sadhus who adhere to him. To such a Guru the disciple appeals: 'I bow down to you, my Master, true friend of the helpless! I pray you to help me cross the terrible ocean of bondage into which I have fallen and by which I am overwhelmed. A mere gracious look from you is a raft that will save me. Oh flowing stream of Grace! I am shaken violently by the winds of a froward fate. I do not know which way to turn. I am tormented by the unquenchable fire of *samsara* that burns around me. I continually pray to you to calm me by the nectar of your Grace. Sadhus such as you abide ever in peace, are great and magnanimous and constantly benefit the world, like the season of spring. Not only have they themselves crossed the ocean of *samsara* but they can calm the fears of others. Just as the world after being heated by the burning rays of the sun is calmed by the cool and gracious rays of the moon, so also it is in your nature to give protection for no reason whatever to people like me who have taken refuge with you from the ocean of *samsara*. Indeed, being helpless and having no other refuge, I have cast on you the burden of protecting me from this *samsara* of birth and death. Oh Lord! the flames of the conflagration of individual being have scorched me; cool me through the outpouring of your gracious words. Your words bring peace, being born of your experience of Divine Bliss. Blessed are they that have even received your gracious glance. Blessed are they that have become acceptable to you. How shall I cross the ocean and what means is there? I do not indeed know what is my fate. You alone must protect me, setting me free from this sorrow of *samsara*.'

The disciple thus takes refuge with the Guru, as enjoined by the scriptures. He waits upon the Guru, unable to bear the burning winds of *samsara*. His mind grows calm through following the Guru's bidding. The Teacher, that is the knower of Brahman, casts upon him his gracious glance and touches his soul inwardly, giving him assurance of protection. 'My learned disciple, have no fear. No harm shall come to you hereafter. I will give you a single mighty means by which you can cross this terrible, fathomless ocean of *samsara* and thus obtain supreme Bliss. By this means world-renouncing sadhus have crossed it and your bondage also shall be destroyed here and now. The scriptures declare: "The means of Liberation for seekers are faith, devotion, meditation, and yoga." You, too, shall obtain these means and if you practise them constantly shall be set free from the bondage to the body caused by ignorance. You are eternally of the form of *Paramatma* and this bondage of *samsara*, of non-Self, has come upon you only through ignorance. It will be utterly destroyed by knowledge born of enquiry into the Self.'

Gazing on the Guru who says this, the disciple asks: 'Oh, Master, what is bondage? How did it come, how does it survive, and how is it to be destroyed ? What is the non-Self? And what, indeed, is the Self? And what is discrimination between Self and non-Self? Graciously bless me with answers to these questions so that, by hearing your replies I may be blessed.'

To this request of the disciple the Master answers: 'Dear soul! if you have felt the desire to be the Self, free from the bondage caused by ignorance, you are indeed blessed. You have achieved life's purpose. You have sanctified thereby your whole line. Just as sons and other relations pay off the debts of a father, so there are others who will free one from bearing a burden on one's head. But the distress caused by hunger can be cured only by eating for oneself, not by others eating for one. And if you are sick you must take medicine and keep a proper diet yourself; no one else can do it for you. Similarly, bondage comes to you through your own ignorance and can only be removed by yourself. However learned a man may be, he cannot rid himself of the ignorance born of desire and fate, except by realizing Brahman with his own infinite knowledge. How does it help you if others see the moon? You must open your eyes and see it for yourself. Liberation cannot be obtained through *Sankhya*, Yoga, ritual, or learning but only through knowledge of the oneness of Brahman and Atma. Just as the beautiful form of the *veena* and the music of its strings only give pleasure to people, but confer no kingdom on them, so also plausible words, clever arguments, ability to expound the scriptures, and the erudition of the learned only give pleasure for the moment. Even study of the scriptures is useless since it does not give the desired result. Once one knows the truth of the Supreme, study of the scriptures becomes unnecessary because there is nothing more to be gained. Therefore one must pass over the great forest of the *sastras*, which only yields confusion of mind, and must instead actually experience the Self through the Guru, who is a knower of Reality. To one who is bitten by the serpent of ignorance, salvation can come only from the elixir of Self-knowledge and not from the Vedas, scriptures, incantations, or any other remedies. Just as a person's sickness is not removed without taking medicine, so too his state of bondage is not removed by scriptural texts such as "I am Brahman" without his own direct experience of the Self. One does not become a king by merely saying: "I am a king" without destroying one's enemies and obtaining the reality of power. Similarly one does not obtain Liberation as Brahman Itself by merely repeating the scriptural text "I am Brahman" without destroying the duality caused by ignorance and directly experiencing the Self. A treasure trove hidden under the ground is not obtained by merely hearing about it but only by being told by a friend who knows it and then digging and removing the slab that hides it and taking it out from below the ground. Similarly one must hear about one's true state from a Guru who knows Brahman and then meditate upon it and experience it directly through constant meditation. Without this, the true form of one's own Self, that is hidden by Maya, cannot be realized through mere argumentation. Therefore those who are wise themselves make every effort to remove the bondage of individual existence and obtain Liberation, just as they would get rid of some disease.

'Beloved disciple, the question that you have put is of the utmost

importance and acceptable to realized souls well versed in the scriptures. It is like an aphorism bearing a subtle meaning and under-
standable to him who craves Liberation. Listen to this reply with a
calm and undisturbed mind and your bonds will be cut asunder at
once. The primary means of obtaining Liberation is *vairagya* (dispassion). Other qualities such as tranquillity, self-control, forbearance, and renunciation of activity can come later, later again the
hearing of Vedantic truth, and still later meditation on that truth.
Finally comes perpetual and prolonged meditation on Brahman.
This gives rise to *nirvikalpa samadhi*, through which is attained the
strength for direct realization of the supreme Self. This power of
direct Realization enables the discriminating soul to experience the
Bliss of Liberation here and now. Such is the *sadhana* leading to
Liberation.

'Now I shall tell you about discrimination between Self and
non-Self. Listen and keep it firmly in mind. Of these two I shall
speak first about the non-Self.

'The brain, bones, fat, flesh, blood, skin, and semen are the
seven factors that constitute the gross body. So say those who know.
The feet, thighs, chest, shoulders, back, head, etc., are its members.
People regard it as "I" owing to the mind's attachment to it. It is
the primary attraction to all, and the most obvious. It is made up
of ether, air, fire, water, and earth which, as the subtle essences,
form sense objects and the groups of five such as sound, touch,
sight, taste, and smell. The ego (*jiva*), being intent on pleasure, regards these as means of enjoyment. Foolish and ignorant persons
are bound to sense objects by the rope of desire, attracted according
to the power of their karma which leads them up and down and
causes them to wander in distress. The serpent and deer die through
attachment to sound, the elephant though attachment to touch, the
moth through attachment to taste, and the bee through attachment
to smell. If these die through attachment to a single sense, what
must be the fate of man who is attached to all five? The evil effects
of sense objects are more harmful than the poison of the cobra,[1]
because poison only kills him who takes it, whereas sense objects
bring destruction to him who only sees them or even thinks of them.
He alone obtains Liberation who, with the sharp sword of detach-

[1] In Tamil this is a play of words, as *vishaya* means sense object and *visha* poison.

ment, cuts the strong rope of love for sense objects and so frees himself from them. Otherwise, even though a man be well versed in all the six *sastras*, he will not obtain Liberation. Desire, like a crocodile, instantly seizes the aspirant after Liberation who tries to cross the ocean of *samsara* and reach the shore of Liberation without firm detachment and straight away drags him down into the ocean. Only that aspirant who kills the crocodile with the keen sword of detachment can cross the ocean and safely reach the shore of Liberation. He who, lacking good sense, enters upon one path after another of attachment to sense objects experiences ever greater distress until he is finally destroyed. But he who exerts control over himself walks on the path of discrimination laid down by the Guru and attains his goal. This indeed is the truth. Therefore if you really want Liberation cast away the pleasures of sense objects as though they were poison. Hold firmly to the virtues of contentment, compassion, forgiveness, sincerity, tranquillity, and self-control. Give up all actions performed out of attachment to the body and strive ceaselessly for Liberation from the bondage caused by ignorance. This body is finally consumed, whether by earth, fire, beasts, or birds. He who, forgetting his real nature, mistakes this body for the Self, gets attached to it and cherishes it and by so doing becomes the murderer of the Self. He who still cares for the body while seeking the Self is like one who catches hold of a crocodile to cross a river. Infatuation with the body is indeed fatal to the aspirant after Liberation. Only he who overcomes this infatuation obtains Liberation. Therefore you too must overcome infatuation for the body and for wife and children and then you will attain Liberation in the supreme state of Vishnu which the great Sages have attained. This gross body is very much to be deprecated, consisting as it does of skin, flesh, blood, arteries and veins, fat, marrow and bones, and is full of urine and excreta. It is produced by one's own past actions out of the gross elements. The subtle elements unite together to produce these gross elements. Thus it becomes a habitation for the enjoyment of pleasures by the ego, like his home for a householder. It is in the waking state that the ego experiences the gross body. It is in this state alone that it can be experienced, when the Self, though really separate from it, is deluded into identifying itself with it and, through the external organs, enjoys the various wonderful gross objects of pleasure such as garlands, sandal paste, woman, etc. Know that the whole of outward *samsara* comes upon the Spirit (Purusha) through the medium of the gross body. Birth, growth, old age, decay, and death are its characteristics. Childhood, boyhood, youth, and old age are its stages. Castes and orders of life are ordained for it. It is also subject to different modes of treatment, to honour and dishonour, and is the abode of various diseases.

'The ears, skin, eyes, nose and tongue are organs of knowledge because they enable us to cognize objects. The vocal organs, hands, feet, etc., are organs of action because they perform their respective modes of action. The internal organ (mind) is single in itself but is variously named mind, intellect, ego, or desire (*chitta*). Mind is the faculty of desire or repulsion. Intellect is the faculty of determining the truth of things. The ego is the faculty which identifies itself with the body as self. Desire (*chitta*) is the faculty that seeks for pleasure. Just as gold and silver are shaped into various forms, so the single life-breath becomes *prana, apana, vyana, udana, samana*. The group of five elements (ether, fire, water, air, earth), the group of five organs of knowledge (ears, eyes, skin, nose, tongue), the group of five organs of action (vocal organs, hands, feet, anus, genitals), the group of five vital airs (*prana, apana, vyana, udana, samana*), the group of the four internal organs (*chitta, manas, budhi, ahankar*), all these together compose the subtle body called the city of eight constituents. Being possessed of desires, it is produced out of the elements prior to their subdivision and mutual combination. The soul has brought this beginningless superimposition upon itself by its own ignorance in order to experience the fruits of its actions. This state of experience is the dream state. In this state the mind functions of its own accord, experiencing itself as the actor, due to its various tendencies and to the effect of experiences of the waking state. In this state the Self, shining with its own light, is superimposed upon the mind without being attached to its actions and remains a mere witness. Just as the axe and other tools of the carpenter are only the means for his activities, so this subtle body is only the means for the activities of the Self which is ever aware. The internal organs perform all their actions owing to the mere proximity of the Self, whereas the Self remains unaffected and untouched by these actions. Good or bad eyesight is due to the state of the eyes, deafness to the ears, and so on; they do not affect the Self, the Knower. Those who know say that inhalation, exhalation, yawning, sneezing, etc. are functions of the life-breath, as also are hunger and thirst. The inner organ (mind), with the light of reflected consciousness, has its seat in the outer organs, such as the eye, and identifies itself with them. This inner organ is the ego. The ego is the actor and enjoyer, identifying itself with the body as "I". Under the influence of the three *gunas* it assumes the three states of waking, dream, and deep sleep. When sense objects are to its liking it becomes happy, when not, unhappy. Thus, pleasure and pain pertain to the ego and are not characteristics of the ever-blissful Self. Objects appear to be pleasant because of the Self and not because of any inherent bliss that is in them. The Self has no grief in it. Its bliss, which is independent of objects, is experienced by everyone in the state of deep sleep and therefore it is dear to everyone. This is borne out by the authority of the Upanishads and by direct perception, tradition, and inference.

'The Supreme (Brahman) has a wonderful *Shakti* (Power or Energy) known as "the Undifferentiated", "Ignorance", "Maya", etc. She is of the form of the three *gunas*. Her existence is inferred by those of understanding from the effects produced by her. She is far superior to all objectivity and creates the entire universe. She is neither being nor non-being, neither does she partake of the nature of both. She is neither composed of parts nor indivisible nor both. She is neither formal nor formless nor both. She is none of these. Such as she is, she is indescribable. She is also beginningless. Yet just as the deluded fear of a snake in a piece of rope is removed by recognizing the rope as such, so too Maya may be destroyed by integral knowledge of Brahman. She has her three gunas which are to be known from their effects. *Rajas*, whose colour is red, is of the nature of activity and is the power of projection. It is the original cause of all activity. From it arise the mental modifications that lead to desires and sorrows. Lust, anger, grasping, pride, hatred, egotism are all tendencies characteristic of *rajas*. This projecting power is the cause of bondage because it creates outward or worldly tendencies. *Tamas*, whose colour is black, is the veiling power. It makes things appear other than what they are. Through its alliance with the power of projection, it is the original cause of man's constant rebirth. He who is enveloped by this veiling power, wise or learned though he may be, clever, expert in the subtle meaning of the scriptures, capable of wonderful achievements, will not be able to grasp the truth of the Self, even though the Guru and others clearly explain it in various ways. Being under the sway of that veiling power, he esteems things which bear the imprint of delusion and ignorance and achieves them. Even though he is taught, he who is enveloped by this veiling power still lacks the clear knowledge and understanding without which it cannot be removed; he always remains in doubt and comes to decisions contrary to the truth. At the same time, the power of projection makes him restless. Ignorance, indolence, inertia, sleepiness, omission of the discharge of duties, and stupidity are the characteristics of *tamas*. One who has these qualities does not comprehend anything but is like a sleeping man or a stone. Now, coming to *sattva*, whose colour is white: although this is quite clear like pure water, yet it gets weak if mixed with *rajas* and *tamas*. The Self shines through *sattva* just as the sun illumines the entire world of matter. Even from mixed *sattva* virtuous qualities result, such as modesty, *yama* and *niyama*, faith, devotion, and the desire for devotion, divine qualities and turning away from the unreal. From the clarity of pure *sattva* results Self-realization, supreme peace, never failing contentment, perfect happiness, abiding in the Self which is the fount of eternal Bliss. The undifferentiated power which is spoken of as a compound of the three *gunas* is the causal body of the soul. Its state is that of deep sleep in which all the sense organs and functions of the mind are at rest. In this state all perceptions cease and the mind in its subtle seed-like form experiences supreme bliss. This is borne out by the universal experience, "I slept soundly and knew nothing".

'The above is a description of the non-Self. These things do not pertain to the Self: the body, the sense organs, the mind, the ego and its modes, happiness due to sense objects, the elements from ether downwards, and the whole world up to the undifferentiated Maya. All this is non-Self. From *mahat* (cosmic intelligence) down to the gross body, everything is the effect of Maya. Know these to be the non-Self. These are all unreal like a mirage in the desert.

'Now I am going to tell you about the real nature of the supreme Self, by realizing which man attains Liberation and is freed from bondage. That realization of "I" is indeed the Self which is experienced as "I–I" shining of its own accord, the absolute Being, the witness of the three states of waking, dream, and deep sleep, distinct from the five sheaths, aware of the mental modes in the waking and dream states and of their absence in the state of deep sleep. That Self sees all of its own accord but is never seen by any of these. It gives light to the intellect and ego but is not enlightened by them. It pervades the universe and by its light all this insentient universe is illumined, but the universe does not pervade it even to the slightest extent. In its presence the body, senses, mind, and intellect enter upon their functions as if commanded by it. By that eternal knowledge all things from the ego to the body, objects and our experience of them, occur and are perceived. By it life and the various organs are set in motion. That inner Self, as the primeval Spirit, eternal, ever effulgent, full and infinite Bliss, single, indivisible, whole and living, shines in everyone as the witnessing awareness. That Self in its splendour, shining in the cavity of the heart as the subtle, pervasive yet unmanifest ether, illumines this universe like the sun. It is aware of the modifications of the mind and ego, of the actions of the body, sense organs and life-breath. It takes their form as fire does that of a heated ball of iron; yet it undergoes no change in doing so. This Self is neither born nor dies, it neither grows nor decays, nor does it suffer any change. When a pot is broken the space inside it is not, and similarly when the body dies the Self in it remains eternal. It is distinct from the causal Maya and its effects. It is pure Knowledge. It illumines Being and Non-being alike and is without attributes. It is the witness of the intellect in the waking, dream, and deep sleep states. It shines as "I–I", as ever-present, direct experience. Know that Supreme Self by means of a one-pointed mind and know "This 'I' is Brahman". Thus through the intellect you may know the Self in yourself, by yourself, and by this means cross the ocean of birth and death and become one who has achieved his life purpose and ever remain as the Self.

'Mistaking the body or not–I for the Self or I is the cause of all misery, that is of all bondage. This bondage comes through ignorance of the cause of birth and death, for it is through ignorance that men regard these insentient bodies as real, mistaking them for the Self and sustaining them with sense objects and finally getting destroyed by them, just as the silkworm protects itself by the threads that it emits, but is finally destroyed by them. For those who mistake the rope for a serpent the integral pure effulgence of the pristine state is veiled by *tamas*, just as the dragon's head covers the sun in an eclipse, and as a result the Spirit (*Purusha*) forgets his reality. He is devoured by the dragon of delusion and, mistaking the non-self for the Self, is overpowered by mental states and submerged in the fathomless ocean of *samsara* full of the poison of sense-enjoyments and, now sinking, now rising, he finds no way of escape. Such are the torments caused by the projecting power of *rajas* together with the veiling of *tamas*. Just as the layers of clouds caused by the rays of the sun expand until they hide the sun itself, so the bondage of ego caused by ignorance in the Self expands until it hides that very Self. Just as frost and cold winds torment one on a wintry day when the sun is hidden by clouds, so too when *tamas* covers the Self the projecting power of *rajas* deludes the ignorant into mistaking the non-Self for the Self and torments them with many sorrows. So it is by these two powers alone that the Self has been brought into bondage. Of this tree of *samsara*, *tamas* is the seed, the "I am the body" idea is the shoot, desire is the young leaf, activity the water that makes it grow, the body the trunk, a man's successive lives the branches, the sense organs the twigs, sense objects the flowers, and divers sorrows caused by activity the fruit. The ego is the bird sitting in the tree and enjoying its fruit.

'This bondage of the non-Self, born of ignorance, causing endless sorrow through birth, death, and old age, is without beginning, yet its complete destruction can be brought about in the way that I will tell you. Have faith in the Vedas and perform all the actions prescribed by them without seeking for any gain from doing so. This will give you purity of mind. With this pure mind meditate incessantly and by doing so you will obtain cognition of the Self. This Self-knowledge is the keen sword that cuts asunder the bonds. No other weapon or contrivance is capable of destroying them, nor wind nor fire nor countless actions.

'The Self is covered over by the five sheaths caused by the

power of ignorance. It is hidden from sight like the water of a pond covered with weeds. When the weeds are removed the water is revealed and can be used by man to quench his thirst and cool him from the heat. In the same way, by process of elimination, you should with keen intellect discard the objective five sheaths from the Self as "not this, not this". Know the Self distinct from the body and from all forms, like a stalk of grass in its sheaths of leaf. Know it as internal, pure, single in its essence, unattached, with no duties to perform, ever blissful and self-effulgent. He who is Liberated realizes that all objective reality, which is superimposed on the Self as the idea of a serpent is on the rope, is really no other than the Self, and he himself is the Self. Therefore the wise aspirant should undertake discrimination between the Self and the non-Self. Of the five sheaths (food, life-breath, mind, intellect, and bliss), the gross body is created out of food, increasing by eating it and perishing when there is none. It is the sheath of food. Compounded of skin, blood, flesh, fat, marrow, excreta, and urine, it is most filthy. It has no existence before birth or after death but appears between them. It undergoes change every moment. There is no law governing that change. It is an object, like a pot, is insentient and has a variety of forms. It is acted upon by other forces. The Self, on the other hand, is distinct from this body and is single, eternal, and pure. It is indestructible, though the body with its limbs is destroyed. The Self is the witness who knows the characteristics of the body, its modes of activity and its three states. It is self-aware and directs the body. Such being the contrast between the body and the Self, how can the body be the Self? The fool thinks of it as the Self. The man of wise action, with some measure of discrimination, takes body and soul together for "I", but the really wise man who conducts the enquiry with firm discrimination knows himself always as the Supreme Brahman, the Being which is of its own nature. The "I am the body" idea is the seed of all sorrow. Therefore, just as you do not identify yourself with your shadow body, image body, dream body, or the body that you have in your imagination, cease also to associate the Self in any way with the body of skin, flesh, and bones. Make every effort to root out this error and, holding fast to the knowledge of Reality as the Absolute Brahman, destroy the mind and obtain supreme Peace. Then you will have no more birth.

Even a learned scholar who perfectly understands the meaning of Vedanta has no hope of Liberation if, owing to delusion, he cannot give up the idea of the non-existent body as the Self.

'Now we come to the vital body of *prana*, which is the life-breath with the five organs of action. The afore-mentioned sheath of food enters upon its course of activity when filled by this vital force. It is nothing but a modification of air, and like air it enters into the body and comes out of it. It does not know its own desires and antipathies or those of others. It is eternally dependent on the Self. Therefore the vital body cannot be the Self.

'The mental sheath is the mind with its organs of knowledge. This is the cause of the wrong concept of the Self as "I" and "mine". It is very powerful, being endowed with diversity of thought forms, beginning with the I-thought. It fills and pervades the vital sheath. The ever-blazing fire of the mental sheath is consuming this whole world, lit by the five sense organs as sacrificial priests, fed by sense objects as the fuel, and kept ablaze by the latent tendencies. There is no ignorance apart from the mind. It is the cause of the bondage of birth and death. With the emergence of the mind everything arises and with its subsidence everything ceases. In the dream state, in which there are no objects, the mind creates its dream world of enjoyers and others by its own powers. Similarly, all that it perceives in the waking state is its own display. It is the experience of all that nothing appears when the mind subsides in deep sleep. Therefore the bondage of *samsara* is only superimposed on the Self by the mind. Actually it has no reality. Just as the wind gathers the clouds in the sky and then disperses them, so the mind causes the bondage but also causes Liberation. The mind first creates in man an attachment to the body and to all sense objects, with the result that he is bound by his attachment like a beast tethered by a rope. Under the influence of *rajas* and *tamas* it is enfeebled and entangles man in desire for the body and objects, but under the influence of *sattva* it breaks away from *rajas* and *tamas* and attains to non-attachment and discrimination and rejects sense objects as though they were poison. Therefore the wise seeker after Liberation must first establish himself in discrimination and desirelessness. The mind is a great tiger roaming wild in the huge jungle of sense objects. Therefore aspirants should keep away from it. It is only the mind that conjures up before the Self subtle and gross objects and all the variations of body, caste, and station in life, qualities and actions, causes and effects. So doing, it tempts and deludes the Self, which is really unattached pure intelligence, binding it by the qualities of body, senses, and life and deluding it with the idea of "I" and "mine" in the fruits of action that it creates. By means of this false representation, the mind creates the myth of *samsara* (bondage) for the Spirit. This is the primal cause of the sorrow of birth and death which binds those who are subject to the faults of *rajas* and *tamas* and lack discrimination. Just as cloud masses revolve through the air, so does the whole world revolve through the delusion of the mind. Therefore those who know Reality declare that the mind is ignorance. He who seeks Liberation must examine his mind by his own efforts and once the mind is purified by such introspection Liberation is obtained and appears obvious and natural. Out of desire for Liberation you should root out all other desires, renounce activity and take to perpetual pre-occupation with Truth (*sravana manana*) which will lead on to perpetual meditation (*nididhyasana*). Then alone can the waves of the mind be stilled. Therefore even this mind sheath cannot be the real Self, since it has a beginning and an end, and is subject to modifications and characterized by pain and grief, and is an object of perception.

'The intellect with the five organs of knowledge is the *vijnana maya* sheath and is also the cause of bondage for the Spirit. It is a modification of the Unmanifest, Beginningless Self which has assumed the form of the ego and conducts all activities through the reflected light of consciousness. It is the conscious agent of activity and its attributes are intelligence and actions. It regards the body and senses as "I" and their mode of life, duties, actions, and qualities as "mine". It performs good or evil actions as dictated by its previous tendencies and as a result of these actions attains to higher or lower regions and wanders there until it is attracted to re-birth in some enticing womb. It experiences the states of waking, dream, and deep sleep and the pleasant and painful fruits of its actions. Within this sheath of knowledge, the Self throbs as the self-effulgent Light, the supreme soul, homogeneous, the Truth, all pervasive, complete, immutable, the Supreme Lord. Yet the Self assumes limitations through the false superimposition of the intellect on it in this sheath, because this is close to it, and in fact the closest of its adjuncts. As a result it is deluded into thinking that it is this sheath. Just as a pot might seem to be different from its clay, so it imagines itself to be different from itself, to be the agent and the enjoyer and seems to be limited in such ways, although it is like the fire in a ball of hot iron, unaffected by the shape of the ball.'

In answer to the Guru, the disciple says: 'Master, I accept your statement that, whether through delusion or not, the Supreme Self has come to regard itself as the ego. But since this superimposition of the ego-concept is beginningless it cannot be supposed to have an end either. How, then, can there be Liberation? But if there is no Liberation the ego-concept becomes eternal and bondage also becomes eternal. Pray enlighten me on this point.'

To this the Master replies: 'That is a good question, my learned disciple. Now listen patiently to my explanation. Whatever has been conjured up by delusion must be examined in the pure light of reason. Things appear real as long as the delusion lasts and perish as unreal and non-existent as soon as it passes, just like the illusion of a serpent seen in a piece of rope and appearing real as long as the illusion lasts. Really the Self is unattached, actionless, characterless, immutable, formless, Being-Knowledge-Bliss, the Inner Witness. It has no sort of relationship with anything. To think that it has is a mere delusion like the appearance of blue in the sky. The false attitude of the ego to the Self is due to the relationship with the beginningless false vehicle, but even this sense of relationship is the result of delusion. Although this attitude of the ego to the Self is without a beginning, that does not make it real. Just as water becomes clear as soon as the dirt is removed from it, so is it with the Self when the effects of the ego and its false adjuncts are dropped from it and ignorance disappears through discrimination between Self and non-Self. Then appears the true self-effulgent Knowledge of the Oneness of God and Self.

'The discarding of the beginningless ignorance with its cause and effects and bodies and states is like the ending of the beginningless non-existence or the ending of a dream when the waking state supervenes. Liberation from the bondage of the false ego concept can never come about except through knowledge acquired by discrimination between the Self and the non-Self. Therefore you also must discriminate in order to remove the non-existent ego. Even this intellectual sheath is subject to change, insentient, a part of a whole, and an object of perception, and therefore it cannot be the Atman. The non-existent can never become eternal.

'Coming now to the sheath of Bliss: this is only a modification of ignorance on which the Supreme Self is reflected. It reveals itself at will in all three states, waking, dreaming, and deep sleep, and yields the different modes of bliss from perceiving, obtaining, and experiencing things. It is experienced effortlessly by all to some extent in deep sleep, but sadhus who have practised discrimination experience the bliss of it perpetually without effort and in its fulness in the deep-sleep state. However, even this sheath of bliss cannot be the Supreme Self, since it is subject to change and possesses attributes. It is the effect of past good deeds and a modification of *Prakriti* and it abides in the other sheaths which are themselves also modifications. If, by the rejection of false ideas, all five sheaths are eliminated, the Self alone is experienced as "I–I". It alone remains, whole and Self-aware, distinct from the five sheaths, the witness of the three states, self-effulgent, immutable, untainted, everlasting Bliss. It is like Devadatta[1] who neither is the pot nor partakes of its nature but is only the witness. The Self is not the five sheaths, which are objects, nor does it partake of their nature, but is a mere witness of them.'

To this the disciple replies: 'Oh Master, after rejecting the five sheaths as unreal, I find nothing remaining except the void, so what is there to be known as "I–I", as the truth of the Self?'

The Guru replies: 'Oh learned one, you are skilful in discrimination and have spoken the truth. The rule of enquiry or perception is: "That which is perceived by something else has the latter for its witness. When there is no agent of perception there can be no question of the thing having been perceived at all." Accordingly, the Self, as awareness, cognizes not only itself but also the existence of the ego with its various modifications of transient names and forms and their nescience. Therefore it is the Self which is their witness. Beyond it there is nothing to know. It is aware of itself through its own effulgence and so is its own witness. It is single

---

[1] A name taken simply as an illustration.

and immutable in the waking, dream, and deep sleep states. It makes itself known as Being-Consciousness-Bliss and is self-effulgent in the heart as "I–I". Through your keen intellect, know this eternal blissful awareness to be the Self or "I". The fool takes the reflection of the sun in the water of a pot to be the sun; the wise man eliminates pot, water, and reflection and knows the sun in the sky as it really is, single and unaffected, but illuminating all three. In the same way the fool, through error and misperception, identifies himself with the ego and its reflected light experienced through the medium of the intellect. The wise and discriminating man eliminates body, intellect, and reflected light of consciousness and probes deeply into his real Self which illuminates all three while remaining uniform in the ether of the heart. Thereby he realizes the eternal witness which is Absolute Knowledge, illuminating all. It is subtle and all-pervasive, neither being nor non-being, with neither inside nor outside, and is self-effulgent. Realizing this, he is set free from the impurities of the ego. He has no more birth or death. He is free from sorrow and becomes the immutable essence of established Bliss. The *Jnani* who, through experience, has realized his Self to be the Brahman as It really is, as Truth, Knowledge, endless Bliss, the Single Essence, eternal, boundless, pure, unattached, and impartible, not only does not return to bondage but is that Brahman Itself, the *Advaita*. That is to say that knowledge of the identity of Brahman and Self is the prime cause of release from bondage. For him who aspires after Liberation there is no other way of release from bondage but knowledge of the identity of Brahman and Self. Therefore you too, by your own experience, know your Self as always "I am Brahman", "Brahman am I", "Brahman alone am I".

'Since there is nothing other than Brahman, It is the supreme *Advaita*. The pot, which is made of clay, has no other form than that of the clay. No one can show the pot except by means of the clay. The pot is only a delusion of the imagination and exists only in name, since it has no other reality than that of the clay. Similarly the whole universe is a superimposition (of form) on the Brahman although it seems to be separate from It. The substratum of Brahman appears through the delusion of the superimposition. The latter is really non-existent, like the serpent seen in the rope. The manifest is only an illusion. The silver seen in the substratum of the mother-of-pearl has no existence apart from it but is the mother-of-pearl itself. Similarly, manifestation has no existence apart from its substratum of Brahman. Whatever, Oh sadhu, appears to the deluded as the manifested world of names and forms, on account of their ignorance and wrong knowledge, whatever objectivity appears as real, all this, when truly realized as it is, is the effect of Brahman, and is superimposed on the substratum of Brahman. Only owing to delusion it appears to be real and it is Brahman, its substratum, which appears to be superimposed on it. Really all these names and forms are nothing at all. They are a myth pure and simple and have no existence apart from their substratum of Brahman. They are nothing but the Being-Consciousness-Bliss which neither rises nor sets. If it were contended that the manifested world has any existence apart from Brahman, that would impair the infinity of Brahman. It would also contradict the authority of the Atharva Veda which declares in unequivocal terms "All this world is indeed Brahman". It would also make out the Omniscient Lord as having uttered a falsehood when He said: "All these elements are not in Me. I, the Indivisible Whole, am not in them." The Mahatmas, who are true sadhus, would not countenance these contradictions. Furthermore, the outer world does not exist in the state of deep sleep and, if investigated, it is seen to be unreal, like the dream world. Therefore any such statement made by fools as that the manifested world has its own existence apart from its substratum of Brahman is as false as the idle words of a man talking in his sleep. It is Brahman Itself which shines everywhere, uniform and complete. This truth the Enlightened (*Jnanis*) know as the One without a second, formless, inactive, unmanifest, never to be destroyed, having no beginning or end. It is Truth, absolute Purity, the essence of pure Bliss. It contains none of the internal differences which are the creation of Maya. It is eternal, continuous, immaculately pure, spotless, nameless, undifferentiated, self-effulgent, beyond the triad of knower-knowledge-known, absolute, pure, unbroken Consciousness, ever shining.

'My beloved disciple, this Self can neither be held nor given up. It is beyond perception and utterance. It is immeasurable, without beginning or end. This Infinity of Brahman is my Self and yours and that of other individuals. Great texts such as "That thou art" reveal the identity between the Brahman known as "That" and the individual known as "thou". The identity is not shown by the literal meaning of "that" and "thou". The literal meaning of "that" is Ishvara's Maya which is the cause of the universe, and the literal meaning of "thou" is the five sheaths of the ego. These are non-existent superimpositions, the cause and effect of non-existent phantoms. Their qualities are opposite to each other, like the sun and the glow-worm, the king and the slave, the ocean and the well, Mt. Meru and the atom. There can be no identity between Brahman and the individual in the literal sense of "that" and "thou", and it is not in this way that the scriptures postulate the identity.

'[The science of the secondary meaning of words is called *lakshana* and is of three kinds. The first is called *jahal-lakshana*, the second *ajahal-lakshana* and the third *jaha-ajahal-lakshana*. In the first the primary sense of a term is rejected and the secondary retained; in the second the primary sense is retained and the secondary rejected; in the third the primary sense is only partly rejected and partly retained.][1] Of these three, we can omit the first two as being of no use for our purpose and take the third. According to this, in a text such as "He is that Devadatta" we eliminate the contradictory aspects of Devadatta manifested at different places and times and concentrate on the identity of Devadatta himself irrespective of place and time. Similarly, in the text in question, we eliminate the non-existent, objective, contradictory attributes of "that" and "thou" as "not this" and "not this" (am I). You can do this on the authority of the Vedas which reject the duality superimposed on Brahman and also by your own intelligence. If attributes such as a shield for a royal person and a badge of ownership for a slave are removed, both alike belong to the genus man. Similarly the text (about "that" and "thou") declares the natural identity between Ishvara and the individual in their residuary aspect of Consciousness apart from the forms of Ishvara and individual. There is no contradiction in this, since Consciousness is the unbroken, single essence of both. Through the word of the Mahatmas, know this blessed identity of Brahman and Self by rejecting as "not I" the non-existent body. Know by your own clear intellect that

[1] This passage in brackets is inserted by the editor.

Brahman is your Self, self-existent, subtle as the ether, ever radiant, true, awareness, bliss, indivisible and whole.

'Truly "thou art That", the Self that is non-dual Brahman, pure and exquisitely serene, the Truth apart from which nothing is. This is so because, even in this waking state, the world and the body with its sense organs and the ego which, owing to ignorance, seems to be separate from the Self, and the life breath are pure myth. "Thou art that" because in the dream state time, space, and objects and the knower of them are all created by sleep and are purely illusory. "Thou art That" because this whole world emanates from Brahman, which alone IS, and is Brahman Itself, just as pots come from clay and are clay itself and indeed are made of clay. That Brahman is untouched by the sixfold changes of birth, youth, growth, old age, decay, and death. It has no caste or custom, tribe or family, name or form. It is without attributes. It has neither merit nor demerit, neither mental nor physical afflictions. It is free from the six evils of hunger, thirst, sorrow, delusion, old age, and death. It has no time, space, or objectivity. It cannot be described by words. The gross mind cannot reach it. It can be comprehended only by the eye of wisdom and experienced in the heart of the Yogi, in his very being, not by the use of any organ. It is the substratum of the illusory world that seems to be superimposed on it. It is the cause of the emanation, preservation, and re-absorption of the world. It is the Supreme Cause, which itself has no cause; all the worlds of name and form are its effects, and yet it is distinct from cause and effect. It is neither existence nor non-existence. Although, owing to delusion, it appears like gold in its varying aspects of name and form and its modifications, yet it has no name or form, no attributes or modifications. It contains no disequilibrium. It is still, like a waveless ocean. It is eternal, formless, spotless, incomparable, ever free, indestructible, pure, without beginning. It is that beyond which there is nothing. It is complete, not compounded of elements or of parts. It is Being-Knowledge-Bliss, uniform, impartible Bliss. It is single in essence. That Brahman which is all this: "That thou art". Meditate on the truth of this in your heart continuously, without break, calmly, with reason and keen intellect. Thus you will obtain essential Knowledge free from doubt, as clear as water in the palm of the hand. Knowledge in the body with its faculties is like a king in the midst of his vast army, and that Knowledge is the Self and is Brahman. Know this by discrimination. Regard all other separate things as This Itself and remain ever as this Self. Thus remaining, you will attain Bliss and peace of Being.

'In the cavity of the Intellect is the single truth of Brahman, distinct from being and non-being. He who remains eternally as that Truth itself is never drawn back again to birth in the body.

'Although a man knows this to be true, the feeling of "I am the doer", "I am the enjoyer" arises strongly in him owing to the bondage (*samsara*) caused by the mighty, beginningless *vasanas* (innate tendencies) which often obstruct him. Curb these tendencies the moment they arise, by your own efforts, by abiding firmly in the Self, by a vision of the Self. Sages such as Vasishta have declared that the withering of the *vasanas* is indeed Liberation. Realization of the Self as It is does not come through tendencies to worldly or sense activity or through prolonged study of the scriptures. To those who seek deliverance from the prison or ocean of *samsara*, the above threefold tendencies are iron fetters say those who are realized. Therefore attachment to the world, the scriptures, and the body must be given up and it must be fully realized that the body is sustained by the force of *prarabdha* (past karma). You should therefore courageously renounce these attachments and strive energetically to overcome *tamas* by the power of *sattva* and *rajas*, then *rajas* through mixed *sattva*, then mixed *sattva* through pure *sattva*. You should do this with a firm and calm mind, helped by the great texts such as "That thou art" which proclaim the identity between the individual self and Brahman. Seek by reasoning and experience to get rid of the *vasanas*, so that you may have firm faith in Brahman and completely root out from the body and senses the feeling of "I" and "mine" which constantly appears as a result of the superimposition. This is to be done by firm abidance in the One Indivisible Self in the Heart and by meditating on the unceasing experience of knowledge of the unity of Brahman and Self thus: "I am not the ego. I am the unceasing Perfection of Brahman experienced as I, the Witness of thought forms.' This meditation must be persisted in until the ego sense is completely rooted out from the body, without a vestige, and the world of individuals appears like a dream. He who meditates has no work to do except beg and perform his natural functions. He must never forget the Self by giving room for worldly speech and sense objects. Agil wood is fragrant by nature, but its fragrance is masked by a bad smell when it comes into contact with water and is revealed when it is rubbed. Constant practice of meditation is this rubbing. The latent tendencies of the mind are removed only to the extent to which it abides in the Self. It is by such constant abidance in the Self that the mind of the Yogi is destroyed. And by the destruction of the mind the outer non-self tendencies of the heart are utterly eradicated. Then the experience of the Supreme Self, which was formerly veiled by the magic of the *vasanas*, shines forth of its own accord like the fragrance of uncontaminated sandal paste.

'In whatever way it may be examined, the ego with all its faculties turns out to be unreal, a momentary limitation, inert, insentient and incapable of realizing the One. The Supreme Self is different from both gross and subtle bodies. It is the witness of the ego with its faculties and exists always, even in deep sleep. The texts say: "It is birthless and deathless." It is immutable and distinct alike from being and non-being. The ego can never be the real Self, the true meaning of "I". Keep aloof from this impure body as you would from an outcast. Give up the sense of "I" in the gross body and all attachments due to the mind, attachments to name and form, tribe and family, caste and social order. Give up also the attachment to the subtle body and its nature and sense of being the doer. Find the feeling of "I" in the Self, which is Truth, Knowledge, and Eternity. Just as the air in a pot is part of the air outside, so conceive of the Self as that self-effulgent Brahman which is the substratum of all, in which the world is seen reflected like a city in a mirror or like shadows cast. Think of yourself as "That I am", without parts, without form, without activity, without duality, unending, Being-Consciousness-Bliss. Know the Self as it really is. Give up this false physical self just as an actor gives up his rôle and remains himself. By knowledge acquired through Self-enquiry discard both microcosm and macrocosm as unreal and, abiding in the unbroken stillness, remain ever at rest in the perfect Bliss as Unqualified Brahman. Thus obtain supreme Peace, which is the purpose of life.

'Though various obstacles contribute to the bondage of the soul, the primary cause of them all is the rising of the false ego-sense. It is through the superimposition of the ego on the Self that this bondage of birth, death and sorrow has come upon you who are by nature Being-Consciousness-Bliss, of boundless glory, eternal, single in essence, unchanging. By nature you have no such bondage. Just as there can be no sound health so long as the effect of a little poison in the body continues, so there can be no Liberation so long as identification with the ego continues. Knowledge of the Identity of the Self with Brahman is clearly revealed as soon as the ego is completely destroyed without residue, together with the illusion of multiplicity caused by the veiling of *tamas*. Therefore, by investigation into the nature of the unattached Self, discover the Truth of your own Self, complete, perfect, self-effulgent and ever blissful. He who is freed from the ego shines eternally as the Self, like the full moon, radiant when delivered from the dragon's head (of eclipse). In the field of the heart the terrible cobra of the ego is coiled round the Bliss of the Self to which it denies access with the threefold hood of the *gunas*. These three fearful heads of the serpent of ego are to be severed, in accordance with the scriptures, only by great courage with the mighty sword of actual experience of the Self. He who has thus destroyed the three-hooded serpent can obtain and enjoy the vast treasure of the Bliss of Brahman. Therefore you, too, give up the I-sense in the ego, which appears like being and assumes that it is the doer, whereas it is only the reflected light of the Self. Turn inwards all the thought-forms that adhere to the ego. He is an enemy of yours, so kill him with the sword of Knowledge. He has been harming you like a thorn in your throat while eating. Give up all desires in order to realize your state as the Supreme Self. Enjoy the kingdom of the Self, be perfect, be still in the stillness of the immutable state of Brahman.

'The ego may in this way be killed, but if thought is given to it even for a moment it revives and engages in activity, driving a man before it as the wind drives winter clouds. Remember that he who associates the I-sense with the body and its faculties is bound while he who does not is Liberated.

'Thoughts of sense objects create a sense of differentiation and thereby cause the bondage of birth and death. Therefore no quarter should be given to the ego, who is the enemy who has such thoughts. Just as a withered lemon tree puts out new leaves if watered, so the ego revives through thoughts of sense objects. The increase of effects makes their seed or cause flourish, while the decay of effects destroys their cause also; therefore you should first destroy the effects. If thoughts, which are the effect, flourish, the ego with its tendencies, which is the cause, also flourishes. From thoughts, outer activities arise, and from these two together the tendencies develop and create the bondage to which souls are subject. In order to escape from this, thoughts, activity, and tendencies must all three be abolished. The best way of doing this is to hold firmly to the view that: "All this that appears as separate names and forms is Brahman Itself." This view must be held to at all times and places and in all states. Firm holding to this attitude reduces activity, and this results in a decline of thoughts, which in turn destroys the latent tendencies. Destruction of the latent tendencies is indeed Deliverance. Therefore develop this helpful tendency to regard everything as Brahman. The result will be that the frail tendencies of the ego will disappear like darkness before the sun. Just as darkness with all its dismal effects disappears before the rising sun, so bondage with all its sorrows will pass away without a trace when the sun of advaitic experience rises. Therefore regard all objective manifestation as Brahman and hold firm in a state of meditation (*samadhi*) and inner and outer beatitude (*nischala bhava*) as long as the bondage due to your past destiny (karma) lasts. While doing so, always remember: "That immovable Bliss of Brahman Itself am I."

'This abidance as Brahman must never be relaxed, for if it is, a false notion of Truth will result which is indeed death, as says Bhagavan Sri Sanath Sujatha, the Son of Brahma. Such a false notion of truth due to swerving from the State of abidance in Truth introduces delusion; from delusion arises the attribution of "I" to the ego and its objects, from this bondage, and from bondage sorrow. Therefore there is no greater misfortune for the Enlightened than wrong understanding and swerving from Reality. Just as water-plants, though removed from a sheet of water, do not stay at the side but cover it over again, so if a man is exteriorized, even though he may be enlightened, if Maya (illusion) once begins to shroud him he will be swayed in numerous ways by the false intellect. This is due to his lapse from watchfulness, his forgetting of his true state, his going out towards sense objects. He is like a man swayed and dominated by a lewd woman, of whom he is enamoured. If, through wrong understanding and swerving from Reality, a man's consciousness slips even the least bit from the target of his own Self, it will enter into outer things and leap from one to another like a ball that slips from your hand and rolls down a flight of stairs. It will begin to consider outer experiences good for it and thence will arise the desire to enjoy them. That will lead to participation in them, which in turn will destroy his abidance in the Self, with the result that he will sink into depths from which he can nevermore arise and will be destroyed. Therefore there is no greater danger in Brahman-consciousness than wrong understanding, which means swerving from one's true state. Only he who has the eternal state of consciousness (*nishta*) obtains Realization (*siddhi*) and so renounces the manifestation (*sankalpa*) born of wrong understanding (*pramada*). Such wrong understanding is the cause of all spiritual decline (*anartha*). Therefore be the *swarupa nishta* who abides ever in the Self.

'He who has attained Liberation in the state of Brahman while still alive will shine so in his bodiless state also. It says in the Yajur Veda: "He who has even the slightest sense of differentiation is always afraid!" He who sees any attributes of differentiation, however small, in the Absolute Brahman will for that reason remain in a state of terror. He who locates the I-sense in the insentient body and its objects, so despised by the various scriptures and their commentaries, will experience sorrow after sorrow like the sinner who commits unlawful acts. We can see from the discrimination between thieves and honest men that he who is devoted to truth escapes misfortune and achieves success, while he who is devoted to falsehood perishes.[1] We also see that shutting out external objects gives the mind a clear perception of the Self, which in turn results in the destruction of the bondage of *samsara*. Therefore the abandonment of all objective reality is the way to Deliverance. If a man discriminates between Truth and non-truth in quest of Liberation and discovers the Truth of the Supreme Lord

[1] This refers to trial by ordeal, placing a hot iron in the hand of a suspected thief, who is burnt if guilty but not if innocent.

through the authority of the scriptures, will he then, like a child, run after non-existent chimera, knowing them to be the cause of his destruction? None would do so. Therefore he who discriminates must also renounce and cease to seek after externals which feed those lower tendencies that cause bondage. He should erase all sorrows due to ignorance by the experience "I am that Supreme Brahman alone, which is Being-Consciousness-Bliss" and should abide ever in his true state, which is Bliss. One who is in the waking state is not dreaming and one who is in the dream state is not waking; the two are mutually exclusive. Similarly, one who is not attached to the body has Deliverance and one who is has not.

'A liberated being is one who sees himself as single and the witness both within and without the world of things moving and unmoving, as the substratum of all. By his universal consciousness experienced through the subtle mind he has removed all the vehicles and he remains as the Absolute Whole. Only such a one is liberated, and he has no attachment to the body. There is no other means of Liberation than this blessed realization that "All is one Self". And this "All is One" attitude is to be obtained by perpetual abidance in the Self and rejection of objects without attachment to them. How can a man reject objective reality if he has the "I am the body" idea and is attached to outer things and always performing actions dictated by them? It is impossible. Therefore renounce all actions based on karma and dharma and, with knowledge of the *tattva*, abide permanently in the Self. Prepare your mind for immersion in perpetual Bliss. This effort will enable you to reject objective reality. It is in order to obtain this *sarvatmabhava* (attitude that all is the Self) that the scriptural text "*Shanto dantha*" (calm and self-controlled) prescribes *nirvikalpa samadhi* (ecstatic trance) for those seekers who have taken a vow of *chandrayana* (regulation of the increase and decrease of food intake through two successive fortnights) and have also performed *sravana* (hearing of the text "That art thou"). A scholar who has not had a firm experience of *nirvikalpa samadhi*, however learned he may be, will not be capable of destroying the ego and its objective reality together with all the accumulated tendencies of his previous births.

'It is the projecting power of Maya together with its veiling power which unites the soul with the ego, the cause of delusion, and, through its qualities, keeps a man vainly dangling like a ghost. If the veiling power is destroyed the Self will shine of itself, and there will be no room either for doubt or obstruction. Then the projecting power also will vanish, or even if it persists, its persistence will only be apparent. But the projecting power cannot disappear unless the veiling power does. Only when the subject is perfectly distinguished from objects, like milk from water, will the veiling power be destroyed.

'Pure discrimination born of perfect knowledge distinguishes the subject from the object and destroys the delusion due to ignorance. The man of discrimination distinguishes the Real from the unreal, reasoning as follows: "Like iron combining with fire, the intellect combines with ignorance to obtain a fictitious unity with the Self which is Being and projects itself as the world of seer, sight, and seen. Therefore all these appearances are false, like a delusion, dream, or imagination. All sense objects from the ego down to the body are also unreal, being modifications of *Prakriti*, subject to change from moment to moment. Only the Self never changes. The Self, distinct from the body, distinct from being and non-being, the witness of the intellect and the meaning implied by the I-sense, single, eternal, indivisible, impartible, is indeed the Supreme Self of eternal Bliss incarnate."

'In this way he discriminates between Truth and untruth and, in doing so, discovers the true Self. With the eye of illumination, he obtains actual realization of the Self and experiences this "I" as the impartible Knowledge of Absolute Brahman. Thereby he destroys the veiling power and the false knowledge and other sorrows that have been created by the projecting power, just as the fear of a snake falls away as soon as one perceives the reality of the rope (that one took to be a snake). Being freed from these ills, he obtains abidance in a state of perfect peace. Thus, only when one obtains realization of the Supreme Identity through *nirvikalpa samadhi* will ignorance be destroyed without vestige and the knot of the heart loosed. How can there be any seed of *samsara* still remaining in the liberated soul who has realized the Supreme Identity with the utter destruction of the forest of ignorance by the fire of knowledge of the Oneness of Self and Brahman? He has no more *samsara*, no more rebirth and death. Therefore the discriminating soul must know the *Atma tattva* in order to be freed from the bondage of *samsara*.

'All forms of creation and imagination appearing as you, I, this, etc., are a result of the impurity of the intellect. They seem to exist in the Absolute, Attributeless Supreme Self, but in the state of absorption (*samadhi*) and experience of Brahman they cease to exist. Also the Self seems to be divisible owing to differences in the vehicles, but if these are removed it shines single and complete. Perpetual concentration is necessary in order to dissolve these differentiations in the Absolute. The wasp's grub that renounces all activity and meditates constantly upon the wasp becomes a wasp, and in the same way the soul that longs for Brahman with one-pointed meditation becomes the Supreme Self through the power of its meditation and perpetual abidance in Brahman, in the Absolute Stillness. So persevere constantly in meditation on Brahman and as a result the mind will be cleansed of the stain of the three *gunas* until it becomes perfectly pure and resumes its true state, when it is ripe for dissolution in Brahman like salt in water. It is like gold being cleansed of its alloy and returning to the purity of its true state through being put in a furnace. Only in such purity of mind can *nirvikalpa samadhi* be obtained, and therewith the essential bliss of Identity. Through this *samadhi* all the knots of the *vasanas* are loosened and all past karmas destroyed so that the Light of the Self is experienced without effort, inwardly and outwardly, and at all places and times. Thus the subtle Brahman is experienced in the single and subtle mental mode of *samadhi* by those of subtle intellect, and in no other way, by no gross outlook, can it be experienced. Similarly the Sage who has inner and outer senses controlled, in solitude and equanimity, obtains experience of the all-pervading Self through perpetual concentration and thus, getting rid of all mental creations caused by the darkness of ignorance, becomes inactive and without attributes and remains eternally in the Bliss of Brahman Himself. Only he is liberated from the bondage of *samsara* who, having obtained *nirvikalpa samadhi*, perceives the mind, senses, and objects, the ears and sound, etc., to inhere in the Self, and not he who speaks only from theoretical wisdom. Brahman can be clearly experienced without any barrier only through *nirvikalpa samadhi*, for apart from that the mental mode always fluctuates, leading from one thought to another. Therefore control the senses and mind and abide firmly in the Self. Utterly destroy the darkness of ignorance and its cause through experience of the One Self and abide ever as the Self. Reflection on truth heard is a hundred times more potent than hearing it, and abiding in it is a hundred times more potent than reflection on it. What limit, then, can there be to the potency obtained through *nirvikalpa samadhi?*

'Restraint of speech, not accepting anything from others, conquest of desire, renunciation of action, continence, and solitude are all aids in the early stages of this *samadhi yoga.* Solitude helps to quieten the senses, and thereby the mind also. Stillness of mind destroys the tendencies and thereby gives perpetual experience of the essential Bliss of Brahman. Therefore the yogi must always exert himself to restrain the consciousness (*chitta*). The breathing must subside into the mind, the mind into the intellect, the intellect into the witness, and by knowing the witness as the fulness of the Unqualified Supreme Self perfect Peace is obtained.

'He who meditates becomes that aspect of his being to which the consciousness is drawn: if to the body, he becomes body, if to the senses he becomes senses, if to the life-breath, he becomes that, if to the mind or intellect, he becomes mind or intellect. Therefore, rejecting all these, the consciousness should subside and obtain peace in Brahman, which is Eternal Bliss.

'Only he who, through desire for Liberation, has attained perfect freedom from desires is able to abide in the Self and get rid of all attachments, inner as well as outer, and he alone achieves inner and outer renunciation. Moreover, it is only he who is without desires, who has perfect non-attachment and so obtains *samadhi* and through *samadhi* the certainty that he has won to *tattva jnana,* which brings Liberation. He who has attained Liberation has attained eternal Bliss. Therefore complete non-attachment is the only path for him who aspires to the bliss of union with the bride Liberation. Non-attachment combined with Self-knowledge wins the kingdom of Deliverance. Non-attachment and Knowledge are like the two wings of a bird needed for ascending the steps to the mount of Deliverance, and if either of them is lacking it cannot be attained. Therefore renounce the desire for things, which is like poison; give up attachment to caste, group, social position, and destiny; cease to locate the I-sense in the body; be ever centred upon the Self; for in truth you are the Witness, the stainless Brahman.

'The Self in the form of Brahman, witness of all finite beings, self-effulgent, shines eternally as I–I in the sheath of *Vijnana*, distinct from the five sheaths. Being experienced as "I", it shines as the true form of the Self, the direct experience, of the great texts. Fix your heart constantly on this Brahman, which is the goal. Let the senses remain in their centres; keep the body steady by remaining indifferent to it; and practise the meditation "I am Brahman, Brahman am I", allowing no other thoughts to come in. Gradually still the mind by practice of the unbroken flow of beatitude. Realize the identity of Self and Brahman and drink the nectar of Brahman Bliss in eternal joy. What use are base thoughts of body and world, which are non-Self? Give up these non-Self thoughts, which are the cause of all sorrow. Hold firm to the Self, the seat of Bliss, as "I" and no longer ascribe the I-sense to the ego and its attributes. Be as indifferent to them as to pots and pictures and meditate perpetually on the Self, which is the cause of Liberation.

'A pot, a huge earthen jar for storing grain, and a needle are all separate things, but when they are cast away there remains only the single expanse of ether. Something which is falsely imagined to exist on the substratum of something else has no reality apart from the real thing, just as a snake imagined in a piece of rope has not. Wave, foam, bubble, and whirlpool if examined are all found to be simply water. Pots of various sizes and shapes are nothing other than clay, and in fact are clay. Similarly, you should reject the limitations of body, senses, life-breath, mind, and ego, which are merely illusory. Only fools perceive and speak of "I", "you", "it" and so forth, out of delusion and folly, being drunk with the wine of illusion (Maya). Even their perception of multiplicity is contained in Being-Consciousness-Bliss, in the perfect purity of Self which, as Brahman, shines as one indivisible whole, like the vast ether. All superimpositions such as body and ego-sense, from Brahma down to a boulder, which are perceived as the world, are really nothing other than the One Self. They are merely the display of *Prakriti* and the Self as pure Being. The one supreme Self, unbroken and homogeneous, exists as east, west, south, and north, inner and outer, up and down, everywhere. He himself is Brahma; he himself is Vishnu, Siva, Indra, gods and men, and everything. What more is there to say? Everything from (the threefold appearance of) Personal God, individual being, and world down to the minutest atom is merely a form of Brahman. In order to remove the superimposition of *mithya* (the false), the scriptures declare "there is no duality at all" (Brahman is One without a second); therefore you yourself are the non-dual Brahman, spotless like the ether, without inner or outer, without attributes, changeless, timeless, without dimensions or parts. What else is there to know? The scriptures declare: "So long as the individual regards the corpse of his body as 'I' he is impure and subject to various ills such as birth, death, and sickness." "Remove all objective reality superimposed on the Self by illusion and know yourself as pure, immutable Siva; then you will become Liberated, the Brahman which is without action and is impartible perfection." The Enlightened who have attained Supreme Knowledge shine as Being-Consciousness-Bliss, homogeneous Brahman, having utterly renounced objective reality. Therefore you, too, reject your gross, impure body and the subtle body that wavers like the wind and the I-sense in them and regard yourself as Being-Consciousness-Bliss, as declared by Vedanta, and thus remain ever as the very Brahman.

'The scriptures declare that: "Duality is of the nature of illusion (Maya) and only non-duality is the Supreme Truth." It is our experience that the diversity created by the consciousness ceases to exist in deep sleep, in which the consciousness is absorbed in bliss. Those who are wise and discriminating know that the proverbial serpent has no existence apart from the substratum of the rope, nor the water of a mirage apart from the mirage. It is our experience that when the mentality assumes the nature of the Self and becomes one with the Attributeless Supreme Self, mental manifestation ceases. All these magical creations which the illusion of the mind sets forth as the universe are found to have no real existence and become untrue when the Truth behind them is realized as Brahman Itself. In the non-dual Brahman the threefold reality of seer, sight, and seen does not exist. It is the substratum into which ignorance, the root cause of the illusion of multiplicity, is absorbed, like darkness into light. Like oceans that endure to the end of the cycle of time, the Truth of Brahman remains single, complete, absolute purity, inactive, unqualified, changeless, formless. Where, then, can be talk of duality or diversity in the homogeneity of Brahman? When in a state of *samadhi* the Enlightened experience in the heart as I-I the homogeneous completeness of that Brahman which is eternal, the bliss of knowledge incomparable, unattached, formless, inactive, unqualified, immutable, characterless, nameless, and free from bondage. It is still, like the ether—and yet nothing can be compared to it. It has no cause and is not an effect. It is beyond imagining. It is to be achieved only through realization of the authority of the Vedanta. The truth of it abides in the heart and is experienced constantly as I. It is neither birth, old age, nor death. In itself it is eternal. It is eternal, tranquil, and undifferentiated; it is vast and still like a calm ocean without a shore. In order not to fall back into *samsara*, practise *nirvikalpa samadhi* by concentration on Brahman, which is experienced in the heart as your own radiant Self free from all limitations and as Being-Consciousness-Bliss. This will destroy the individual consciousness which is the cause of all error, and thus you can unravel the knot of the heart which causes the ills of birth and death. Thus will you obtain the glory of unbroken bliss and become one who has experience of the Self, and by doing so achieve the purpose of human life, a boon so rare to obtain.

'The Self-realized Yogi, knowing his true nature, the great Mahatma, shows his wisdom by rejecting his body, regarding it as a corpse, as the mere shadow of his being, existing only owing to past destiny. Such a great Mahatma knows himself to be the unbroken bliss of the Self. He has utterly consumed the body and its attributes in the fire of Brahman, which is eternal, immutable Truth. Having thus consumed his body and remaining with his consciousness ever immersed in the ocean of bliss which is Brahman, he himself is eternal Knowledge and Bliss. How then should he care to nourish or sustain his body or be attached to it, feeding as he does on the eternal nectar of Brahman, inwardly and outwardly? Just as the cow does not care about the garland round its neck, so too he does not care whether the body, bound by the strings of past karma, lives or dies. So you too reject this inert, impure body and realize the pure and eternal Self of wisdom. Give no more thought to the body. Who would care to take back what he has once vomited?

'Knowledge of a mirage keeps one away from it, and ignorance that it is a mirage leads one to seek it. Similarly, knowledge leads to the path of return and ignorance to worldly pursuits. The achievement of Self-knowledge or Self-realization frees a man from the ills arising from error and brings him eternal content and unequalled bliss eternally experienced; ignorance, on the other hand, pushes him into objective experience of error and misery. How, then, should the wise man who has severed the knot of the heart with the sword of wisdom continue to perform the various vain actions which occupied him during the time of his delusion? What cause could induce him to activity?

'Knowledge leads to non-attachment; solitude and abandonment of home lead to Knowledge; the bliss of Self-experience and tranquillity results from solitude and abandonment of home. If these results are not obtained step by step, the previous steps become invalid. The perfection of non-attachment is when previous tendencies to seek enjoyment no longer arise. The perfection of Knowledge is when the I-sense no longer pertains to the body. The perfection of solitude is when thoughts subside through perpetual striving and, dissolving in Brahman, no longer turn outwards.

'Do not differentiate between Self and Brahman or between world and Brahman. On the authority of the Vedas realize "I am Brahman". Attain the pure beautitude of Oneness and establish the pure consciousness immovably in Brahman so that you become dissolved in Brahman. Being ever Brahman, renounce objective reality and let your enjoyments be witnessed or known by others, like the state of sleeping children. Renounce activity and, with the purity of Primal Being, abide in eternal enjoyment of pure Bliss. Although your mind is dissolved and you are like one forgetful of the world, remain ever awake, and yet like one who is not awake. Remain indifferent to the body and senses and outer things that follow you like a shadow. Be one who discriminates, free from the stain of *samsara* and from tendencies and sense objects. Retain consciousness without thought. Retain form, though formless. Have no likes and dislikes in what is experienced at the moment and no thought of what may happen in the future. Give up all thought of inner and outer and concentrate permanently on the blissful experience of Brahman. Through the power of knowledge maintain perfect equanimity in face of all opposites such as vice and virtue, likes and dislikes, or praise and blame whether by sadhus or by the wicked. The dedicated Sage is like a river emptied into the ocean, untouched by the attack of sense objects, absorbed in the Self, and it is only such a one who attains realization while still in the body. He alone is worshipful and reaps the reward of worthy actions. All his innate tendencies have been destroyed by his knowledge of Identity with Brahman and no renewal of *samsara* can be ascribed to him. Just as even the most lustful person never thinks of enjoying his own mother, so the Sage who experiences the perfection of Brahman never turns back to *samsara*. If he does, then he is not a Sage who has known Brahman but only an outward-turning soul.

'Identity with Brahman is the fire of knowledge which burns up *sanchitha karma* (destiny stored up for future lives) and *agamya karma* (destiny being created in this life). *Sanchitha karma* is destroyed because it can no longer cause birth in higher or lower worlds once the Sage has awakened from the illusion of activity in which he harvested merit and demerit through countless ages. And *agamya karma* can no longer affect him because he knows himself to be established as the Supreme Brahman, indifferent as the ether to the effects of karma. There is ether in a pot containing alcohol, but is it affected by the smell of the alcohol? Not at all. Having spoken of the *sanchitha* and *agamya karma* of the Sage, it now remains to explain how his *prarabdha karma* (that part of past karma which is to be experienced in this life) is also a myth. Although ever absorbed in his true state, he is sometimes seen to experience the fruits of his past actions or to take part in outer activity; so people say that he is not free from karma since he must reap the good and bad effects of past action. Does not the rule that there is fruit of past action where there is destiny and no fruit where there is no destiny apply to the Sage also? They argue: if one shoots an arrow at an animal, thinking it to be a tiger, but it later turns out to be a cow, can the arrow be recalled? Once shot, it will certainly have to kill the cow. So too, they say, destiny that started on its course prior to the dawn of Enlightenment must produce its effects, so that the Sage is still subject to *prarabdha karma* only and must experience its effects. However, the scriptures

declare such *prarabdha* to be unreal, because a man who has awakened from a dream experience does not go back into the same dream
or desire to cling to the dream experiences or the body and environment of the dream as "I" and "mine". He is perfectly free from the
dream world and happy in his awakened state, whereas a man who
retains any attachment to the dream cannot be said to have left the
state of sleep. In the same way, one who has realized the Identity of
Brahman and Self sees nothing else. He eats and excretes but as
though in a dream. He is beyond all limitations and associations.
He is the Absolute Brahman Itself. The three kinds of karma do not
affect him in the least, so how can one say that only *prarabdha karma*
affects him? Is one who has awakened still dreaming? Even if it were
said that *prarabdha karma* affects the Sage's body, which has been
constructed from the result of past karma, that would only affect him
so long as he had the "I am the body" idea, but once that is gone,
prarabdha cannot be attributed to him, since he is the Self, not born
of karma, beginningless, pure, and described by the scriptures as
"unborn, eternal, and deathless". But to attribute *prarabdha* to the
body, which is unreal and a figment of illusion, is itself an illusion.
How can an illusion be born, live, and die as Reality? It may be asked
why, then, should the scriptures refer to a non-existent *prarabdha*?
It may also be asked how the body can continue to exist through
knowledge after the death of ignorance and its effects. To those who
are so misguided and under the influence of false ideas the explanation is given that the scriptures admit that the Sage has illusory
prarabdha only as a concession for the sake of argument and not to
postulate that the Sage has a body and faculties. In him is visible the
eternally established state of non-dual Brahman, beyond mental or
verbal description and definition, without beginning or end, integral
Being-Consciousness-Bliss, established, motionless, changeless,
measureless, multiple, unattached, homogeneous, never to be
rejected or obtained, subtle, inwardly and outwardly complete, with
no substratum, beyond the *gunas*, without colour, form, or change,
as pure Being. Nothing at all is to be seen there of what obtains
here. It is only by knowledge of this Oneness in the heart through
Atma Yoga, by renouncing enjoyment and the very desire for
enjoyment, that dedicated Sages who have peace and self-control
obtain Supreme Deliverance.

'Therefore, my son, if you, too, by the eye of wisdom obtained through unwavering *samadhi*, discover beyond all doubt the Supreme Self of perfect bliss which is your original nature, you will no longer have any doubts about what you have heard. Cast out, therefore, the delusion created by the mind and become a Sage, a Realized Man who has attained the purpose of life. The Teacher, like the scriptures, gives instructions common to all, but each person must experience bondage and deliverance, hunger and satisfaction, sickness and health for himself; others can only infer it from him. Similarly, he who discriminates must cross the ocean of birth and death by his own efforts through the grace of the Supreme Lord. Thus obtaining release from bondage, which is due only to ignorance, remain as Being-Consciousness-Bliss. The scriptures, reason, the words of the Guru, and inner experience are the means you have to use for this.

'The essence of the Vedantic scriptures may be condensed into the following points:

'First: In me, the unmoving Brahman, all that seems different is utterly without reality. I alone am. This is called the standpoint of reason.

'Second: The dream and all else that appears in me as the result of magic is an illusion. I alone am the Truth. This is called the standpoint of non-existence.

'Third: All that appears as form apart from the sea, that is the bubble and the wave, is the sea. All that is seen in a dream is in him who sees the dream. Similarly, in me as in the ocean or the man who dreams, all that seems separate from me is myself. This is called the standpoint of absolute dissolution.

'Reject the outer world by any of these three means and recognize him who sees it to be infinite, pure, homogeneous Brahman, Who is the Self. He who has thus realized Brahman is Liberated. Although all three of these viewpoints are aids to Realization, the third, in which one conceives everything as one's own Self, is the most powerful. Therefore, knowing the impartible Self to be one's own Self, by one's own experience, one must abide in one's own true nature, beyond any mental form. What more is there to say? The whole world and all individuals are really Brahman, and abidance as that impartible Brahman is itself Deliverance. This is the essence and conclusion of all the Vedas. The scriptures are the authority for this.'

The disciple realized the truth of the Self through these words of the Guru, through the authority of the scriptures and by his own understanding. He controlled his sense organs and, becoming one-pointed, remained for a short time absorbed in unswerving *samadhi* in that Supreme Self. Then he rose up and spoke thus to his Guru:

'Oh Master of the Supreme Experience, incarnation of the Supreme Peace, of Brahman, of the eternal essence of non-duality, endless ocean of grace, I bow down to you.'

Then, prostrating, he begins to tell of his own experience: 'Through the grace of the blessed sight of you the affliction due to the evil of birth is over and in an instant I have attained the blissful state of Identity. By realization of the identity of Brahman and Self my feeling of duality has been destroyed and I am free from outer activity. I cannot discriminate between what is and what is not.[1] Like the iceberg in the ocean, I have become absorbed bit by bit into the ocean of the Bliss of Brahman until I have become that ocean itself, whose nature and extent my intellect fails to plumb. How can one conceive of the vastness of this ocean of Brahmic Bliss full of the Divine Essence, how describe it in words? The world that was perceived a moment ago has entirely vanished. Where has it gone, by whom has it been removed, into what has it been dissolved? What a wonder is this! In this vast ocean of Brahmic Bliss full of divine experience, what is there to reject or accept, to see, hear or know apart from its own Self? I alone am the Self of Bliss. I am unattached; I have neither a gross nor a subtle body. I am indestructible; I am perfect stillness; I am neither the doer nor the enjoyer; I undergo no change. Action is not mine. I am not the seer or the hearer, the speaker, the doer, or the enjoyer. I am neither things experienced nor things not experienced but he who illumines both. I am the Void, within and without. I am beyond compare. I am the Spirit of old. I am without beginning. There is no creation in me of "I" or "you", of "this" or "that". I am both within and without all the elements as the conscious ether in them and also as the substratum on which they are. I am Brahma, I am Vishnu, I am

[1] This does not imply that the disciple is in a state of ignorance, unable to differentiate between Reality and illusion, but, on the contrary, that he is now established in the Non-duality beyond all opposites, even the opposite of being and non-being.

Rudra, I am Isa, I am Sadasiva. I am beyond Isvara.[1] I am the all-comprehensive witness, the indivisible, homogeneous Brahman, infinite, eternal, Being itself, unbroken whole perfection, existence, eternal, pure, enlightened, liberated, and of supreme Bliss. What were formerly experienced as separate things and as experiencer-experience-experienced I now find to be all in myself. Even though the waves of the world arise owing to Maya, as a wind rises and subsides, they arise and subside in me who am the unbounded ocean of Bliss.

'Fools who are condemned for their errors wrongly ascribe body and other ideas to me who am harmless and immutable. It is like dividing illimitable, formless time into parts such as year, half-year and season. Just as the earth is not made wet by the waves of a mirage, so destruction cannot touch me in any way, for I am un-attached like the ether, separate from all that I illumine, like the sun, motionless as a mountain, boundless as the ocean. Just as the ether is unaffected by the clouds, so am I by the body; how then can it be my nature to wake, dream, and sleep, as the body does? It is only the bodily limitations (upon Being) that come and go, act and reap the fruits of action, that are born, exist, and dissolve. How can I perform karma, choose activity or withdrawal, reap the fruits of merit or demerit, I who am like the fixed mountain mentioned in the Puranas, who am ever motionless, indivisible, complete and perfect, like the ether, who am one perfect whole without senses, consciousness, form, or change? If a man's shadow is cold or hot or has good or evil qualities, that does not affect the man at all; and in the same way I am beyond virtues and vices. The scriptures also declare this. Just as the nature of a house does not affect the light within it, so too objective characteristics cannot affect me who am their witness, distinct from them, changeless, and untouched. Just as the sun witnesses all activity, so am I the witness of this whole objective world. Just as fire pervades iron, so do I permeate and enlighten the world; and at the same time I am the substratum on which the world exists like the imaginary serpent in a piece of rope. Being the self-effulgent "I", I am not the doer of anything nor he who causes it to be done; I am not the eater nor he who causes anything

[1] Even Isvara, the Personal God, is a condensation or manifestation of Absolute Being and therefore to some extent a limitation. Even this is transcended in the State without impurities, without any ego-sense.

to be eaten; I am not the seer nor he who causes anything to be seen.

'It is the superimposed adjunct that moves. This movement of the reflected consciousness is ascribed by the ignorant to the objects reflected. So too, they say that I am the doer, the enjoyer, that I, alas, am them. Being inactive like the sun (in causing growth upon earth), being the Self of the forms and elements, I remain untouched by the reflected light of consciousness. It makes no difference to me if this body drops down on earth or in water. The qualities of the reflected light of consciousness no more affect me than the shape of a pot affects the ether inside it. States and functions of the intellect such as doing, enjoying, understanding, being dull-witted or drunk, bound or liberated, do not affect me since I am the pure non-dual Self. The duties (*dharmas*) arising from *Prakriti* in their thousands and hundreds of thousands no more affect me than the shadows cast by clouds affect the ether. I am that in which the whole universe from *Prakriti* down to gross matter appears as a mere shadow, that which is the substratum, which illumines all, which is the Self of all, is of all forms, is all pervasive and yet distinct from all, that which is all void, which is distinct without any of the attributes of Maya, that which is scarcely to be known by the gross intellect, which is ether itself, which has neither beginning nor end, which is subtle, motionless, formless, inactive, immutable, that pure Brahman in its natural state, unbroken, eternal, true, aware, endless, self-subsistent Bliss, non-dual Brahman.

'Master, I was perplexed in the nightmare forest of *samsara*, of birth, old age, and death, caused by Maya, distressed by the tormenting episodes in it and terrified by the tiger of the ego. You awakened me from that nightmare by your grace and saved me, bringing me supreme Bliss. Master of great experience, by the glory of your grace even I have obtained the empire of Real Being. I have become blessed and have accomplished the purpose of this life. Redeemed from the bondage of birth and death, I realize the reality of my being, which is the entire ocean of Bliss. Oh, it is all the glory of your grace, Oh Lord of Masters! Obeisance again and again to your blessed feet which, being in the form of the pure bliss of consciousness, are seen as the whole of creation. Obeisance for ever and ever!'

The Lord of Masters is thus addressed with jubilant heart by the disciple who bows at his feet after realizing the truth of the One Being, the supreme Bliss. He replies: 'Just as he who has eyes has nothing to do but delight in forms, so he who knows Brahman has no other satisfying use for his intellect than experience of the Brahman Reality. Who would enjoy looking at a painted moon when the full moon shines in all its splendour for our delight? No one who has true knowledge can give up the essence to find delight in what is unreal. There is neither satisfaction nor banishment of sorrow in the experience of unreality; therefore a man must make every effort to see with the eye of realization and with the mind in a state of perfect peace, to see his own Self as Brahman, as the truth of non-duality shining as the Self of the whole universe. He must meditate on this and concentrate ceaselessly on the Self. Then he will enjoy unbroken experience of essential Bliss and this alone will satisfy him. It is the intellect which causes restlessness, appearing as a city in the clouds in the attributeless whole of the conscious Self, and so the intellect must achieve absolute stillness and this will give eternal bliss and serenity in Brahman. When stillness and silence have been attained there will be contentment and peace. Perfect silence free from latent tendencies is the only means of experiencing eternal bliss for the Mahatma, for him who knows Brahman, who has realized the Self and experiences unbroken bliss.

'The Sage who has thus realized the Supreme Brahman will ever delight in the Self with unobstructed thought-current. He comes and goes, stands, sits, and lies down, performs whatever actions he will, with no need to observe place, time, posture, direction, rules of *yama*, or other stages of yoga, or positions for concentration. What need is there for rules such as *yama* for realizing one's Self? No external discipline is needed to know one's Self as "I am Brahman", just as "Devadatta"[1] needs no outer technique to know himself as such. This ever-existent Self shines of its own accord when the mind is pure, just as a pot is naturally seen when the eyesight is not defective. There is no need to consider the purity of place or time for abiding in the Self. Just as the world is illumined by the sun, so all the universes and the Vedas, Shastras, Puranas, and various elements are illumined by Brahman, who is also consciously self-

[1] Taken here simply as a specimen name.

effulgent. How can this Brahman be illumined by any low non-existent non-self? This supreme Self is self-effulgent with manifold powers (*shakti*), incapable of being known by anyone, and yet is experienced by everyone as the "I-I" in the heart. It is in realizing this Atman that the knower of Brahman is released from bondage, and when released he knows the contentment of experiencing the essence of eternal Bliss. The perfection of his beauty is beyond imagining. He feels no happiness or sorrow on account of outer condditions, whether agreeable or disagreeable, and has no likes or dislikes. He accepts like a child all conditions that surround him owing to the desires of others. Just as an innocent boy is absorbed in his game without worrying about hunger, thirst, or physical distress, so is the Sage absorbed in the play of his own Self without ego-consciousness and delights permanently in the Self. Ascending in the chariot of his body, he who enjoys the wide expanse of pure consciousness begs his food without any thought or feeling of humiliation, drinks the water from rivers, wraps himself in cloths that have not been washed or dried, or in the bark of trees, or goes naked. No code or rule of conduct binds him, for he is permanently free. Although sleeping on the ground, like a child or madman, he remains ever fixed in Vedanta. Mother earth is the flowery couch on which he lies. He sleeps without fear in the forest or cemetery, for his sport and pleasure are in Brahman. He who is the universal Self assumes at will countless forms and has countless experiences. In one place he behaves like an idiot, in another like a learned man, and in a third like one deluded. Again, in one place he moves about as a man of peace, in another as a king, in another as a beggar eating out of his hand for want of a bowl. At one place he is seen to be adored, at another decried. Thus he lives everywhere and the Truth behind him cannot be perceived by others. Although he has no riches he is eternally in bliss. Although others may not help him he is mighty in strength. Although he may not eat he is eternally satisfied. He looks on all things with an equal eye. Though acting, it is not he who acts; though eating, it is not he who eats; though he has a body he is bodiless. Though individualized, he is the One Indivisible Whole. Knowing Brahman and liberated while yet in the body, he is not affected by likes and dislikes, joys and sorrows, auspicious and inauspicious things, natural to the common man who is attached to the body. Although the sun is never really caught by the dragon's head, (in an eclipse) it seems to be, and fools who do not know the truth say: "Look! the sun is caught." Similarly they say that he who knows Brahman has a body, but that is their delusion, because although he seems to have a body he is in no way affected by it. The body of the Liberated Man, although free from bondage, exists in one place or another, like the sloughed skin of a snake. The body of a Liberated Man, like a log of wood tossed up and down by the current of a river, may sometimes be immersed in pleasure owing to his *prarabdha*, but even though this is so, due to the effects of latent tendencies in *prarabdha*, as with the body of a worldly person, he still remains the witness in his state of inner silence, the hub of the wheel, free from desire and aversion and utterly indifferent. He neither attaches the senses to the objects that give pleasure nor detaches them. The fruits of his actions do not affect him in the slightest, since he is completely drunk with the unbroken experience of the nectar of bliss. He who knows Brahman is the Absolute Self, the Supreme Lord, with no need for special forms of meditation. Of this there is no doubt.

'He who knows Brahman has achieved the purpose of life and is eternally liberated as Brahman, even though living in the body and using its faculties. Indeed, he realizes the state of Brahman even with the destruction of the body and its adjuncts. It is like an actor on the stage who is the same individual whether he wears a mask or not. It makes no difference to a tree whether the place where its dead leaf falls is auspicious or not, whether it is a river, a canal, a street, or a temple of Siva. Similarly, it does not affect the Sage where his body, already burnt in the fire of Knowledge, is cast away. The Being-Consciousness-Bliss of the Self does not perish with the body, breath, intellect, and sense organs any more than a tree does with its leaves, flowers, and fruit. The scriptures also declare: "Only that which is finite and mutable can perish," and also: "The Self, which is established consciousness, is Truth and is imperishable." The Sage is Brahman in the perfect Bliss of Non-duality; he is established in Truth, which is Brahman. How, then, can it matter where and when he sheds his body, which is a vehicle of skin, flesh, and impurities? Getting rid of the body, the staff, and the water-pot (of the mendicant) is not really Liberation; Liberation as understood

172 THE COLLECTED WORKS OF RAMANA MAHARSHI

by the Sages really means loosing the knot of ignorance in the heart.

'Just as a stone, a tree, a straw, grain, a mat, pictures, a pot, and so on, when burned, are reduced to earth (from which they came), so the body and its sense organs, on being burnt in the fire of Knowledge, become Knowledge and are absorbed in Brahman, like darkness in the light of the sun. When a pot is broken the space that was in it becomes one with space; so too when the limitation caused by the body and its adjuncts is removed the Sage, realized during life, shines as Brahman, becoming absorbed in the Brahman he already was, like milk in milk, water in water, or oil in oil, and is radiant as the One Supreme Self. Thus, when the Sage who abides as Brahman, which is Pure Being, obtains his disembodied absolute state he is never again reborn. How can there be rebirth for a Sage who abides as Brahman, his body and its limitations burnt by the fire of Knowledge, the Identity of individual and Supreme. The existence of all that is either affirmed or denied in the one substratum of the indestructible, eternal, unattached, non-dual, absolute Self depends only on the mind, just as the appearance or disappearance of the imaginary snake in a piece of rope has no basis in reality. Bondage and Liberation are creations of Maya, superimpositions upon the Brahman, imagined by the mind without any existence in reality. It is a fool who blames the sun for his blindness. It is impossible to argue that bondage (*samsara*) is caused by the veiling power (*tamas*) of Maya and Liberation by its destruction, since there is no differentiation apart from Maya. Such an argument would lead to a denial of the truth of Non-duality and an affirmation of duality. This would be contrary to the authority of the scriptures. How can there be any display of Maya in non-dual Brahman, which is perfect stillness, One Whole like the ether, spotless, actionless, unstained, and formless? The scriptures even proclaim aloud: "There is in truth no creation and no destruction; no one is bound, no one is seeking Liberation, no one is on the way to Deliverance. There are none Liberated. This is the absolute truth." My dear disciple, this, the sum and substance of all the Upanishads, the secret of secrets, is my instruction to you. You also may impart it to one who aspires after Liberation, only be careful to examine him several times to make sure that he has real detachment and is free from all the sins and impurities of this dark age.'

On hearing these words from the Guru, the disciple bows down to him several times and then takes leave and goes home in a state of bliss. The Master also, immersed in the ocean of Bliss, wanders about the land in order to purify it.

Thus has been revealed the true nature of the Self in the form of a dialogue between the Guru and his disciple, as any who seek Liberation can easily understand. May these useful instructions be followed by those who have faith in the authority of the scriptures and who aspire after Liberation, by those advanced seekers who perform their prescribed duties without caring for the fruits of their actions and have thus cleansed themselves of mental impurities, who are not attached to the comforts of *samsara* and who have attained a state of equanimity.

Souls wandering about in the wild and terrible forest of *samsara* are oppressed by the torment of thirst caused by the terrific heat of the threefold evil, and are then deluded by the mirage of water. The great Master Shankara Bhagavath Padacharya wishes to inform them of the existence close at hand of an ocean of sweet water, the bliss of Non-duality, so that they may obtain relief, and has blessed them with his Vivekachudamani, 'The Crest Jewel of Wisdom' which will confer on them the eternal bliss of Liberation. This is beyond doubt.

OM
Peace, Peace, Peace.

II

Drik Drisya Viveka

Translated and with introductory verse by

BHAGAVAN SRI RAMANA MAHARSHI

O Thou Divine Sankara,
Thou art the Subject,
That has Knowledge
Of subject and object.
Let the subject in me be destroyed
As subject and object.
For thus in my mind arises
The Light as the Single Siva.

*   *   *   *   *

ALL our perception pertains to the non-Self. The immutable Seer is indeed the Self. All the countless scriptures proclaim only discrimination between Self and non-Self.

The world we see, being seen by the eye, is *drisya* (object); the eye which sees is *drik* (*subject*). But that eye, being perceived by the mind, is *drisya* (object) and the mind which sees it is *drik* (subject). The mind, with its thoughts perceived by the Self, is *drisya* (object) and the Self is *drik* (subject). The Self, cannot be *drisya* (object), not being perceived by anything else. The forms perceived are various, blue and yellow, gross and subtle, tall and short, and so on; but the eye that sees them remains one and the same. Similarly, the varying qualities of the eye, such as blindness, dullness and keenness, and of the ears and other organs, are perceived by the mind singly. So, too, the various characteristics of the mind, such as desire, determination, doubt, faith, want of faith, courage, want of courage, fear, shyness, discrimination, good and bad, are all perceived by the Self singly. This Self neither rises nor sets, neither increases nor decays. It shines of its own luminosity. It illumines everything else without the need for aid from other sources.

Buddhi, as the sum total of the inner organs, in contact with the reflected consciousness has two aspects. One is called egoity and the other mind. This contact of the *buddhi* with the reflected consciousness is like the identity of a red-hot iron ball with fire. Hence the gross body passes for a conscious entity. The contact establishing identity between the ego and the reflected Consciousness is of three kinds:

1. The identification of the ego with the reflected Consciousness is natural or innate.

2. The identification of the ego with the body is due to past karma.

3. The identification of the ego with the Witness is due to ignorance.

The natural or innate contact continues as long as the *buddhi*, but on Realization of the Self it proves to be false. The third-mentioned contact is broken when it is discovered by experience that there is no sort of contact of anything at all with the Self, which is Being. The second-mentioned contact, that born of past karma, ceases to exist on the destruction of the innate tendencies (*vasanas*). In the deep sleep state, when the body is inert, the ego is fully merged (in the causal ignorance). Its being half manifest is the dream state, and its being fully manifest is the waking state. It is the mode or modification of thought (with its latent tendencies) that creates the inner world of dreams in the dream state and the outer world in the waking state. The subtle body, which is the material cause of mind and ego, experiences the three states and also birth and death.

Maya of the causal body has its powers of projecting (*rajas*) and veiling (*tamas*). It is the projecting power that creates everything from the subtle body to the gross universe of names and forms. These are produced in the *Sat-Chit-Ananda* (Being-Consciousness-Bliss) like foam in the ocean. The veiling power operates in such a way that internally the distinction between subject and object cannot be perceived, and externally that between Brahman and the phenomenal world. This indeed is the cause of *samsara*. The individual with his reflected light of Consciousness is the subtle body existing in close proximity with the Self that is the *vyavaharika* (the empirical self). This individual character of the empirical self appears in the Witness or *Sakshin* also through false superimposition. But on the extinction of the veiling power (*tamas*), the distinction between witness and the empirical self becomes clear; and the superimposition also drops away. Similarly, Brahman shines as the phenomenal world of names and forms, only through the effect of the veiling power which conceals the distinction between them. When the veiling ends, the distinction between the two is perceived, for none of the activities of the phenomenal world exist in Brahman.

Of the five characteristics: Existence, Consciousness, Bliss, name and form, the first three pertain to Brahman and name and form to the world. The three aspects of Being, Consciousness and Bliss exist equally in the five elements of ether, air, fire, water and earth and in devas (gods), animals, men, etc., whereas the names and forms are different. Therefore, be indifferent to names and forms, concentrate on Being-Consciousness-Bliss and constantly practise *samadhi* (identity with Brahman) within the heart or outside.

This practice of *samadhi* (identity with Brahman) is of two kinds: *savikalpa* (in which the distinction between Knower, Knowledge and Known is not lost) and *nirvikalpa* (in which the above distinction is lost). *Savikalpa samadhi* again is of two kinds: that which is associated with words (sound), and meditation on one's own consciousness as the witness of thought forms such as desire, which is *savikalpa samadhi* (internal), associated with (cognizable) objects. Realizing one's own Self as 'I am Being-Consciousness-Bliss without duality, unattached, self-effulgent', is *savikalpa samadhi* (internal) associated with words (sounds). Giving up both objects and sound forms of the aforesaid two modes of *samadhi* and being completely absorbed in the Bliss experienced by the realization of the Self is *nirvikalpa samadhi* (internal). In this state is obtained steady abidance, like the unflickering flame of a light kept in a place free from wind. So also, in the heart, becoming indifferent to external objects of name and form and perceiving only Being of (or as) *Sat* is *savikalpa samadhi* (external) associated with objects; and being aware continually of that *Sat* (true existence) as the unbroken single essence of Brahman is *savikalpa samadhi* (external) associated with words (sound). After these two experiences, Being which is uninterrupted like the waveless ocean is *nirvikalpa samadhi* (external). One who meditates should spend his time perpetually in these six kinds of *samadhi*. By these, the attachment to the body is destroyed and the mind that perpetually abides in the Supreme Self (*Paramatman*) wherever it may wander is everywhere spontaneously in *samadhi*. By this constant practice of *samadhi*, the Supreme Self, who is both highest and lowliest, who encompasses *Paramatma* as well as *jivatma*, is directly experienced, and then the knot of the heart is loosed; all doubts are destroyed and all karmas (activities) cease too.

Of the three modes of individual being: the limited self (as in deep sleep), the empirical self (as in the waking state) and the dreaming self, only the individual limited by the deep sleep state is the true Self (*Paramarthika*). Even he is but an idea. The Absolute alone is the true Self. In reality and by nature he is Brahman itself, only Superimposition creates the limitations of individuality in the Absolute. It is to the *Paramarthika Jiva* that the identity of *Tat Twam Asi* (That thou art) and other great sentences of the Upanishads applies, and not to any other. The great Maya (the Superimposition without beginning or end) with her veiling and projecting power (*tamas* and *rajas*) veils the single impartible Brahman and, in that Brahman, creates the world and individuals. The individual (*jiva*), a concept of the empirical self in the *buddhi*, is indeed the actor and enjoyer and the entire phenomenal world is its object of enjoyment. From time without beginning, till the attainment of Liberation, individual and world have an empirical existence. They are both empirical. The empirical individual appears to have the power of sleep in the shape of the veiling and projecting powers. It is associated with Consciousness. The power covers first the individual empirical self and the cognized Universe, and then these are imagined again in dream. These dream perceptions and the individual who perceives them are illusory, because they exist only during the period of dream experience. We affirm their illusory nature, because on waking up from dream no one sees the dream objects. The dreaming self experiences the dream world as real, while the empirical self experiences the empirical world as real but, when the *Paramarthika Jiva* is realized, knows it to be unreal. The *Paramarthika Jiva*, as distinguished from those of the waking and dream experiences, is identical with Brahman. He has no 'other'. If He does see any 'other', He knows it to be illusory.

The sweetness, liquidity, and coldness of water are characteristics present equally in waves and the foam. So, too, the Being-Consciousness-Bliss character of the Self (the aforementioned *Paramarthika*) is present in the empirical self and through him in the dream self also, because of their being only illusory creations in the Self. The foam with its qualities such as coldness subsides in the waves; the waves with their characteristics such as liquidity subside in the water, and the ocean alone exists as at first. Similarly, the dream self and its objects are absorbed in the empirical self; then the empirical world with its characteristics is absorbed in the *Paramarthika* and, as at first, Being-Consciousness-Bliss which is Brahman shines alone.

OM TAT SAT

Sri Ramanarpanamasthu

Note on Pronunciation

The vowels in the transliteration here used have rather the Continental than the English values. They are approximately as follows:

a   as in father
e   between e in ten and ai in wait
i   between i in bid and ee in meet
o   between o in hot and or in short
u   between u in put and oo in shoot
ai as igh in night
ou as in pound.

The consonants are pronounced as in English, with the following exceptions:

1. A consonant between v and w but approximating more to v is transliterated by some writers as v and by others as w, as for instance in the two forms Isvara and Iswara.

2. A consonant between s and sh but approximating more to sh is transliterated by some writers as s and by others as sh, as for instance in the two forms Isvara and Ishvara.

This consonant is used in both Siva and Vishnu, but it has become usual to transliterate it as s in the former case and sh in the latter, and therefore that usage is followed here.

3. The words jnani and jnana are pronounced approximately as gnyani and gnyana.

4. h after a letter other than s or c does not change the letter but is slightly aspirated.

Glossary

A

Advaita: Non-duality, often incorrectly termed 'monism'.

Agamya Karma: Actions good and bad of the present life, expected to bear fruit in future births.

Aham: I; embodied self; soul.

Aham Sphurana: The throb of Self-Bliss in the heart.

Aham Svarupa: One's true nature.

Ahamkara (or ahankara): The ego-self.

Ajnana: Ignorance; knowledge of diversity.

Ananda: Bliss.

Anartha: Evil, worthless.

Antahkarana: Instruments of inner perception.

Antarmukha drishti: Inward vision.

Apana: One of the ten vital airs.

Aprana: Beyond manifest life; devoid of life.

Asana: Yogic posture.

Ashtanga-Yoga—Yoga consisting of eight stages of discipline.

Atma (or Atman): Self; principle of life and sensation.

Atma Dhyana ⎫
Atmanusandhana ⎬ Contemplation on the Self.

Atma Vichara: Inquiry into the Self.

Avidya: Nescience, ignorance.

B

Bhagavan: A commonly used name for God. A title used for one like Sri Ramana who is recognized as having realized his identity with the Self.

Bhahirmukha drishti: Outward turned consciousness.

Bhakta: A devotee.

Bhakti: Devotion and love.

Bharata: A form of address used by Sri Krishna towards Arjuna in the Bhagavad Gita, meaning a shining soul.

Bhavana: Continued meditation: steady concentration of mind.

Brahma: Lord of Creation. God as the Creator.

Brahman: The Absolute.

Buddhi: Intellect; one of the four aspects of the internal organ.

C

Chakra: A wheel, a Yogic centre of concentration.

Chandrayana: Expiatory fast for a full month, commencing from the full moon, food being diminished every day by one handful during the dark fortnight, and increased in like manner during the bright fortnight.

Chit: Absolute Intelligence or Consciousness.

Chitta: The mental mode turned towards objects. That aspect of the mind in which impressions are stored.

D

Dahara Vidya: Contemplation of the deity in the cavity of the heart.

Deva: A god or celestial being.

Devata: A deity.

Devi: The Divine Mother or a Goddess.

Dharma: Virtuous deeds: harmonious life; a man's natural duty. Also inherent qualities.

Dhyana: Contemplation; the seventh rung in the ladder of eightfold yoga.

Drik: Subject.

Drisya: Object.

G

Ganapati: The elder son of Siva, the remover of obstacles. The same as Ganesha, the Chief of Siva's hosts.

Gudakesa: An epithet of Arjuna for having conquered sleep. Lord Krishna uses this term in addressing Arjuna.

Gunas: The three fundamental qualities, tendencies, or stresses which underlie all manifestation; *sattva*, *rajas*, and *tamas*, characterized as white, red, and black respectively.

H

Homa: Sacrifice in fire.

Hridayam: The Heart (*Hridi* + *Ayam* = centre this.) The seat of Consciousness at the right side of the chest, as experienced and expounded by Bhagavan Sri Ramana.

I

Indra: The Lord of the devas. The first student of *Brahma vidya*. The Divine Mother was his Teacher.

Isa: The Supreme Lord.

Iswara (Ishvara): The name of the Supreme Lord indicating his lordship of the worlds.

J

Jaganmaya: The mystery of the world.

Jiva: The individual soul or ego.

Jivan Mukta: One who has realized the Supreme Identity while still in the body.

Jivan Mukti: Deliverance while yet in this life.

Jnana: Knowledge of the Absolute transcending form and formlessness.

Jnana Marga: The path of Knowledge.

Jnani: A Self-realized Man, a Sage; one who has attained Realization by the Path of Knowledge.

K

Kailas: A mountain in the Himalayas reputed to be the abode of Siva.

Kaivalya: Absolute Oneness. Final emancipation. One of the 108 Upanishads.

Kali yuga: The last of the four ages of the world, namely *Krita, Treta, Dwapara,* and *Kali. Kali* is reckoned as having begun in 3102 B.C.

Kama: Desire. Physical love.

Karma: Action, work, deeds. Also fruits of action accumulating in three ways as *sanchita, prarabdha,* and *agami,* which see. Also destiny.

Karma Marga: The path of ritual, religious duties, and action.

Kevala Kumbhaka: Retention of breath leading to stilling of the mind, without inhalation or exhalation.

Kshetra: A sacred place of pilgrimage, a shrine. In Yoga, city, or the field of body.

Kshetrajna: The conscious principle (Knower) in the field of the body. The absolute witness aware of the three states of the self—waking, dream, and sleep.

Kundalini: The mystic circle of three and a half coils situated in the umbilical region. The Yogic principle of serpent power. The Primal Maya.

L

Laya: Absorption. In Yoga absorption of breath and mind in the heart.

M

Maharshi (Maha Rishi): Great Rishi or Sage.

Mahat: The intellectual principle as source of *ahankara*, which see. From the Absolute emanates the Unmanifest, from it *Mahat*, and from *Mahat* the *ahankara*.

Mahatma: A lofty soul; highly spiritual person; Master in tune with the infinite.

Mahavakya: The four main sentences, proclaiming the Truth of Brahman, one each from the Itareya (Aitareya) Upanishad of Rig Veda, Brihadaranyaka of Yajur Veda, Chandogya of Sama Veda, and Mandukya of Atharva Veda. Also one of the 108 Upanishads explaining the Maha Vakyas.

Maheswara: One of the five aspects of Lord Siva, as veiling the Truth from souls, till their karma is completely worked out. Also, Siva as Para-Brahman, the Absolute Being.

Manana: Contemplation. The second of the three stages of Vedantic realization.

Manas: Mind, reason, mentality. Also used for the aggregate of *chitta*, *buddhi*, *manas*, and *ahankara*.

Mantram (Mantra): Cosmic sound forms of the Vedas, used for worship and prayer. Also seed letters for meditation on the form of the Lord. Ritualistic incantation.

Marana: The art of causing death through supernatural powers.

Math: A meeting place and abode of Sadhus.

Maya: Illusion, false appearance. Manifestation or Illusion personified.

Mithya: The false.

Moksha: Liberation; final emancipation; release from transmigration.

Mouna: Silence. The Inexpressible. Truth of Brahman, expressed by the Brahman-knower by His mere abidance in stillness.

Mudra: Hand pose in worship and dance.

Mukta: A liberated man.

Mukti: Liberation.

Mutt: *See* math.

N

Nadi: The 72,000 nerves of the body conveying the life force. Of these, *Ida*, *Pingala*, and *Sushumna* are three main ones. In the state of *samadhi* all of them are merged in the single '*Para*' or '*Amrita*' *Nadi*.

Nasha: Destruction.

Nididhyasana: The last of the three stages of Vedantic realization. Uninterrupted contemplation.

Nirasa: Desirelessness.

Nirvikalpa Samadhi: The highest state of concentration, in which the soul loses all sense of being different from the Universal Self, but a temporary state from which there is return to ego-consciousness.

Nischala Bhava: Immobility; steadfastness. Also Eternity.

Nishta: Abidance in firm meditation.

Niyama: Discipline: religious duties as ordained for the second of the eight stages of Yoga.

P

Padma: Lotus; in Yoga, a posture in which the right foot is placed on the left thigh and the left foot on the right thigh with proper hand pose.

Paramapada: The Supreme state.

Paramarthika: The true Self.

Paramatma: The Supreme Self, the Universal Brahman.

Parantapa: An epithet of Arjuna, meaning he who destroys his enemy.

Partha: Arjuna, the son of Pritha—another name for Kunti, his mother.

Prajnana Ghana: Brahman; the Absolute, immutable Knowledge.

Prakriti: Primordial Substance out of which all things are created. The Primal Nature.

Pramada: Swerving from abidance in the Absolute.

Prana: The first of the ten vital airs centred in the heart.

Pranava Japa: Incantation of Om.

Pranayama: Breath control.

Prarabdha Karma: That part of one's past karma whose effect is due to be worked out in this life.

Prasthana Traya: The triple canon of Vedanta. The three Vedantic scriptural authorities: Upanishads, Brahma Sutras, Bhagavad Gita.

Pratyahara: Withdrawal of the senses from objectivity: the fifth rung in the ladder of Yoga.

Puranas: Eighteen sacred books ascribed to Vyasa, dealing with primary and secondary creation, genealogy of kings, etc.

Purnam: Fulness, Plenum, Infinite.

Purusha: Spirit, soul, the living principle.

Purushartha: Human ends; objectives worthy of human pursuit, *Dharma*, *Artha*, *Kama*, and *Moksha*.

R

Raghava: An epithet of Sri Rama as belonging to the line of Raghu.

Raja Yoga: The principal system of Yoga as taught by Patanjali.

Rajas: One of the three primal qualities, described as red, the principle of activity. (*See* guna).

Rishi: Sage. (*See* also Maharshi).

Rudra: Siva in one of his five aspects. God as Destroyer.

S

Sada Siva: The Supreme Lord as eternal goodness.

Sad-Guru: The Great Master, the true or perfect Guru.

Sadhana: A path towards Liberation.

Sadhu: An ascetic or one who has renounced the world in quest of Liberation.

Sahasradala: The thousand petalled lotus; the centre of illumination experienced in the crown of the head on the Yogic path.

Sakshin: Witness.

Samana: One of the ten vital airs.

Sanchitha Karma: Accumulated Karma of former births that still remains to be experienced.

Sankalpa: Volition, mental activity, thought, tendencies, and attachments.

Sankhya: One of the six systems of Indian philosophy.

Sannyasa: Renunciation.

Sannyasin: One who has renounced the world.

Santodanta: One who is calm and self-controlled.

Sarvatma Bhava: The state of experiencing the Self as all. Abidance in the Oneness of Being.

Sastras: Scriptures.

Sat: Existence. Pure Being.

Satchidananda: Being-Consciousness-Bliss.

Sattva: Tendency to purity; one of the three gunas (which see).

Savikalpa samadhi: A state of consciousness in which the distinction between Knower, Knowledge, and Known is not yet lost.

Shakti (or Sakti): The manifesting energy of a Divine Aspect, represented mythologically as the wife of a God.

Siddha: One endowed with supernatural powers and capable of performing miracles. One who has accomplished the end.

Siddhi: Realization, attainment. Also supernatural powers.

Siva The Supreme Lord, also one of the Hindu Trinity.

Sivoham: The incantation: 'I am Siva.'

Skanda: The younger Son of Siva; the leader of the divine hosts. The same as Subramanya.

Smriti: Authoritative Hindu scriptures other than the Vedas (*Sruti*).

Sraddha: Earnestness, faith, a faithful acquisition of theoretical knowledge of Truth.

Sravana: Hearing of the Truth, from the Master.

Sruti: Vedas, heard by the Sages in their transcendental state, and transmitted to disciples by word of mouth.

Sushupti—Deep sleep.

Svarupa Nishta: Abidance in the Self.

T

Tamas: Darkness, ignorance; one of the three gunas (which see).

Tanmaya Nishta: Abidance in the Self.

Tapas: Religious austerities.

Tat: That, Brahman.

Tattva jnana: Knowledge of Brahman or Atman.

Tattvam: Reality; Truth; principle.

Tat-Tvam-Asi: 'That thou Art'.

Turiya: The fourth state; the witness Consciousness—ever present and unchanging as against the changing states of waking, dreaming, and deep sleep.

U

Udana: One of the ten vital airs, having its seat in the neck.

Upadesa: The Spiritual guidance or teaching given by a Guru.

Upanishads: Philosophical writings forming part of the Vedas.

V

Vaikunta: The heaven of Vishnu.

Vairagya: Freedom from worldly desires; dispassion.

Vasanas: Predispositions, tendencies, or propensities of the mind in the present life, due to the experiences of former lives.

Vasudeva: Lord Krishna, as the son of Vasudeva, the Lord whose manifestation all this world is. One of the 108 Upanishads showing the path of Vasudeva.

Veda: The sacred books of the Hindus: Rig, Yajur, Sama, and Atharva, revealed through the Rishis.

Vedanta: The Absolute Truth as established by the Upanishads, Brahma Sutras, and Bhagavad Gita as interpreted by Sri Vyasa. The end or consummation of the Vedas.

Veena: A string instrument.

Vichara: Enquiry into the truth of the Self.

Videhamukta: A Liberated Being after he has left the body.

Videhamukti: Self-Realization after leaving the body.

Vijnana: Knowledge; discriminating the real from the unreal.

Vijnanamarga: The path of discriminate Knowledge.

Vishnu: God as preserver. One of the Hindu Trinity.

Vishya vasanas: Predisposition towards sense enjoyments.

Viveka: Discrimination.

Viyoga: Separation.

Vyana: One of the ten vital airs, causing the circulation of blood and pervading all the body.

Vyaraharika: The phenomenal or empirical.

Y

Yama: The first rung in the ladder of the eightfold Yoga; Self control; abstention from lying, killing, theft, lust, covetousness, etc.

Index